Helping Your Kids Deal with
ANGER,
FEAR, and
SADNESS

H. NORMAN WRIGHT

HARVEST HOUSE PUBLISHERS

EUGENE, OREGON

Cover by Terry Dugan Design, Minneapolis, Minnesota

HELPING YOUR KIDS DEAL WITH ANGER, FEAR, AND SADNESS
Copyright © 2005 by H. Norman Wright
Published by Harvest House Publishers
Eugene, Oregon 97402
www.harvesthousepublishers.com

Library of Congress Cataloging-in-Publication Data

Wright, H. Norman
　Helping your kids deal with anger, fear, and sadness / H. Norman Wright.
　　p. cm.
　Includes bibliographical references.
　ISBN 0-7369-1333-5 (pbk.)
　1. Child rearing—Religious aspects—Christianity.　2. Anger in children—Religious aspects—Christianity.　3. Fear in children.　I. Title.
　BV4529.W733 2005
　248.8'45—dc22　　　　　　　　　　　　　　　　　　　　　　　2004020852

Printed in the United States of America

05 06 07 08 09 10 11 12 13 / VP-MS / 10 9 8 7 6 5 4 3 2 1

Contents

The Roller Coaster
of Emotions

Over the past 30 years of working with parents in counseling and seminars, the most frequently raised questions I have been asked involve anger:

> "Why does my child get so angry? Can't he learn to control that temper?"
>
> "He's like a volcano ready to explode. What can I do?"
>
> "She won't listen when she gets angry."
>
> "What can I teach my child about anger? How can I help him?"
>
> "Is this reaction normal?"

More than any other emotion, anger in a child's life is a big concern for parents. And unfortunately, most children do not have positive models for what to do with their anger. Some children have no control over it, while others are too controlled.

There is so much for all of us to learn about anger: where it comes from, how to talk about it, how to express it in a healthy and nondestructive way, and what the Word of God has to say about it.

One of the reasons for writing this book is to help children learn about some of their emotions at an early age. By doing this, they could have a more emotionally balanced adolescence and adulthood. During my many years of counseling, I have spent too much time helping adults learn things about their emotions that could have been learned as a child. Hence, the reason for this book: to help you help your children, whether toddlers or teens, deal with their emotions in a healthy manner. And in the process, you could learn something about yourself as well.

Our main focus will be on anger. There is so much concern over this volatile emotion and so much to learn. From there, we are going to explore the fears of children and how to help them triumph over fear and worry. If this can be accomplished at an early age, they can experience so much more from their life.

Do children get depressed? Yes, they do, and it can be serious. I have included chapter 9 so you can identify the indications of depression.

Finally, there is a foundational chapter that speaks to your child's identity in Christ. Here you will discover how this is intertwined with your child's emotions.

I hope you find this resource helpful as you fulfill your calling by God to be a parent who nurtures every part of your child's life.

1
The Problem with Anger

"My teen could be called the 'time-bomb kid.' He can go off at any moment. The problem is we don't know when the timer has run out. There's no predicting when he'll explode."

"I think my child came from the Old West. He was one of those who carried a six-gun with a hair trigger. The slightest pressure and boom—it went off. It's the same way with Tim, only it's his angry outbursts. Other kids would take it in stride. Not Tim, he goes off."

The angry child—it is not a pretty sight. Life is tough at times. It is tough for kids, teens, and parents. All of us experience anger at one time or another. But some children seem to have a lit fuse burning all the time. And unfortunately, that fuse is way too short. An angry child also seems to have the ability to trigger this emotion in those around him or her. An angry child has the ability to shape other people's attitudes and behaviors toward him. Being around an angry child necessitates walking on eggshells so you do not step on a land mine and set off an angry tirade. And because of the responses he receives from other people, he transfers thoughts and expectations about others into new situations. Often he creates a self-fulfilling prophecy.

Studies have identified a number of characteristics that shape the way angry children view life and respond to adversity. It is much easier to help your children learn how to deal with their anger the younger they are.

Anger distorts the way we view our world around us. You know what I mean. What are the thoughts that flow through *your* mind when you are angry? Are they pleasant and rational? Probably not. And we, as adults, are supposed to have greater control than children.

Many children are resilient and come back to an even keel after their episode of anger. But some *prefer* living with anger. To them, conflict seems to be the norm rather than peace and harmony. Why the difference?

First of all, let's identify your children to see where each falls on the anger scale:

| Calm & peaceful | Occasional anger | Some anger | Angry much of the time | Constant anger |

Place the name of your child (or children) on this scale.

Any children listed on the right side of the scale tend to have a number of common traits. Perhaps these descriptions are familiar to you.

Angry children create their own problems. By the way they behave, they create issues and even see problems that do not exist. They lack insight into their contribution to the problem. They are good at blaming. Some expect other people to see them as a problem. These children need a calm response and a parent who says, "I believe you can change. I believe you can do it differently. Let's talk about what you'll do differently next time."

Secondly, angry children have a difficult time understanding the problems they create. Not only that, trying to calm them down just does not work. Many of them don't want to talk about what happened. Why? Because they know you want them to see their role in this situation, and who wants to admit they did anything? So they avoid talking about it.

The memory of an angry child is selective. They remember what you or another person did and somehow develop amnesia for their part. Dr. Tim Murphy describes the pattern well: "Each time you try to get an angry child to rethink the problem, he starts with his conclusion using distorted thinking to circle back to support that conclusion."[1]

One of the tendencies for anyone who is angry is to confuse feelings with facts. If a child or teen acts on feelings, it is quite easy to move into an angry response.

A third characteristic is blaming other people for their outburst. Who causes the anger? Other people. "If I lost my temper, you caused it." It is a great way to avoid responsibility for their feelings, their reactions, and any damage. An angry child is a hurting child, and who causes the hurt? Other people. The child can respond to people in unacceptable ways which bring negative reactions. Angry children do not see their part in creating their problems. How do you respond when your child is sullen or sarcastic or angry? However you react can be misinterpreted, and you are the "bad guy." Even nice responses can be misinterpreted by an angry child.

A fourth characteristic is taking any bad feeling and turning it into a mad feeling. It is as though angry children only allow one feeling into their life: anger. Fear is turned into anger. Hurt is turned into anger. Frustration is turned into anger. And when anger is there, the response can be "Act! Attack!"

One parent handled this by saying, "Susan, I can see you're angry. If we couldn't call this anger, what other word from this list could we use?"

mad	furious	riled-up
cranky	burned-up	hot
annoyed	crabby	grumpy
snarly	ornery	mean
bitter	raging	resentful
ticked-off	bugged	out-of-control

Another characteristic of angry children is their lack of understanding of the feelings of other people. And why not? If they cannot understand their own, how can they have empathy for the feelings of other people? As a child grows in his understanding of himself, he will be better able to connect with other people.

It makes sense that angry children attack other people rather than solve problems. What better way to protect themselves than by attacking other people? To them, anger seems to be the best response regardless of the consequences. The best word to describe some angry children is *mean*. They hurt other people maliciously and intentionally.

Power. This is what angry children generally want. Many discover that anger gets them what they want, so why not use it? One of their best power tools is words.

> Death and life are in the power of the tongue, and they who indulge in it shall eat the fruit of it [for death or life] (Proverbs 18:21).

Reckless words pierce like a sword (Proverbs 12:18a NIV).

Another powerful characteristic of angry children is no surprise. Because their words to other people are so destructive, what they say to themselves is just as destructive. We all talk to ourselves. It is normal. Our self-talk can be positive or negative. Perpetually angry children have refined the ability to carry on arguments in their mind. They spend time rehearsing conversations, which then feeds their anger and aggression. Before you say anything, you are the enemy.

Parents can talk with their children about self-talk and assist them in creating positive conversations that can lead to positive responses. It takes patience and constant work, but it can be effective.[2]

More about that later. What you have just read describes the *angry child.* There is a difference between this one and a child who experiences anger. And the latter is what most of us parents are dealing with. Before you can help your child, you need to understand what we are talking about…and that is anger.

Anger. That controversial, misunderstood word. That controversial, misunderstood emotion! It affects all of us, yet continues to baffle us, especially when it erupts from our children. If we are going to help them, we need to understand what it is and how to deal with it.

Even the so-called experts disagree. Some say, "Experience it and express it." Others say, "Disown it and repel it." It is a part of us whether we like it or not. We were created with the capacity to become angry. And so was your child. Remember the first time his face turned red, his stomach stuck out, and his fists clenched? Was that a pretty sight? Did you jump up and down for joy or just say, "Oh, great"?

Well, what is anger? One dictionary defines *anger* as "a feeling of strong displeasure." Is that your definition, or do you couch it in other terms? How would *you* describe anger? The dictionary definition suggests that anger is manageable, that is like so many other feelings—neither right nor wrong in itself. The problem lies in its mishandling. Why should we expect our kids to handle anger well? Most adults have problems dealing with it constructively.

Some children express their anger like a heat-seeking missile. There is no warning. No alarm sounds. Everything has been calm. And then the missile explodes. The damage? Wounded feelings and distanced relationships. You are upset. They are upset. The recovery from the onslaught can take days or even longer. Do you have a missile-launching child?

On other occasions, anger is like a snake, gliding silently and unseen through the underbrush. It may raise its head, promising a commitment, but then it disappears once more, its promise forgotten. The bite of this anger is not as blatant or devastating as the missile, but the results can be similar: "What, Mom? Oh, I didn't hear you," or "You thought I would clean my room? Oh, I didn't know that. When did you tell me?" (The next chapter will identify this style of anger).

Too often we link any expression of anger with an explosion. Have you noticed the major synonyms used for *anger? Wrath, rage, fury, hostility.* These words paint a picture of anger as out of control and running wild. They reflect anger that is destructive. Some of us equate anger with our memories of the old comic book and television hero "The Incredible Hulk," an out-of-control, raging beast—anger uncontrolled. On the other hand, some people would like to maintain a staid emotional composure like Mr. Spock, the emotionless Vulcan from *Star Trek.* He never allowed himself to be angry. Anyone come to mind in your home? It could be a child or an adult.

Often anger begins slowly in a child. It starts as a slight arousal, a feeling of discomfort. Jimmy is sitting there and he does not like what his sister said. He begins to notice changes in his body—especially a feeling of tension. His pulse rate increases, and there is a surge of adrenaline. He is now angry. You have felt it, too, and so have I. That is how anger starts.

The Many Faces of Anger

Anger wears many faces. Look at the examples in Scripture. Anger is not new. It was there in the beginning. Moses was livid with the Hebrew people when they set up idol worship. With the energy provided by his anger, he was able to regain control of the people. David was consumed with anger when Nathan told him about the rich man stealing from the poor man. He used this anger to face his own pride and admit his own sin. Anger can be used in a creative way to resolve major social problems. But do children use it wisely? Not usually.

In the early chapters of the Gospel of Mark, we find the Pharisees looking for ways to find fault with Christ. One day, Christ entered a synagogue and noticed a man with a withered hand. The Pharisees watched His every move to see if Christ would heal the man. Christ turned to the man and said, "Rise and come forward!" He turned to the Pharisees and asked, "Is it lawful to do good or to do harm on the Sabbath, to save a life or to kill?" They would not answer Him.

"After looking around at them with anger, grieved at their hardness of heart, He said to the man, 'Stretch out your hand.' And he stretched it out, and his hand was restored" (see Mark 3:1-5 NASB). Christ felt and expressed anger at the injustice of the

Pharisees. He was frustrated by the fact that they held their rigid orthodoxy to man-made rules as more important than the suffering of another man.

An injustice involves the violation of that which is moral or right, the rights of another person, or your own personal rights. It almost always produces feelings of anger.

The Problem with Anger

Anger does not wear a happy face; it wears an ugly face. Let's consider some of the destructive results of this emotion. People seem to go to extremes in their demonstration of anger, either outwardly or inwardly. Turn it outward too much, and it destroys other people. Turn it inward too much, and it destroys us.

Not only did Cain misuse this emotion, but so did Esau, Saul, the Pharisees, Attila the Hun, Adolf Hitler, and certain other rulers in many countries of the world. Our history is a tragic drama of hostility and domination. We have seen it recently at schools like Columbine.

Did you know anger is a motivator? It can motivate you to hate, wound, damage, annihilate, despise, scorn, loathe, vilify, curse, ruin, and demolish. When we are angry, we might ridicule, get even with, laugh at, humiliate, shame, criticize, bawl out, fight, crush, offend, or bully another person. All of these do very little to build relationships. That is the problem with anger and its damaging behavior.

The first time we see the effects of anger in Scripture, they are very destructive. "But on Cain and his offering he did not look with favor. So Cain was very angry, and his face was downcast. Then the LORD said to Cain, 'Why are you angry?'" (Genesis 4:5-6 NIV).

Cain was angry at his brother because Abel's sacrifice was acceptable and his was not. Inwardly, Cain experienced anger, and the result was the first murder (Genesis 4:8). Cain was alienated from his brother, from other people, and from God. His anger led to murder and to extreme loneliness.

Almost everything in life has a price tag. Go into any store and rarely will you find anything that is free. Purchasing a new car may give us a feeling of elation, comfort, and prestige, but it costs. Expressing our anger can be a relief, and it can influence or even control a situation, but it, too, has a price tag. Some of the costs may be obvious, such as a strained relationship (resistance or withdrawal of other people when we come near them). Children and parents can be alienated by anger. Even though there are personal costs to anger, the greatest price to be paid is that between us and our child.

Our anger carelessly expressed will override the love, care, and appreciation that creates close relationships with our children. The person who has a reputation for anger is soon given a wide berth. Indeed, the Book of Proverbs recommends, "Make no friendships with a man given to anger, and with a wrathful man do not associate, lest you learn his ways and get yourself into a snare" (22:24-25). Do you know anyone who fits this description?

Here, Scripture is describing a hothead, a person who fires up at the drop of a hat. Perhaps this is how your child responds to anger.

Anger can be a very upsetting emotion. You may be afraid of your own anger because you have seen people totally out of control with this emotion. They did not just experience anger; they raged. Perhaps you believe that healthy people do not have anger. Or perhaps you feel that you do not have the right to be angry at other people. How you process anger is repeated in your child. Let's consider what the Bible has to say about anger.

The Word of God has much to say about anger, and it uses a number of words to describe the various types of anger. In the

Old Testament, the word for anger actually meant "nostril" or "nose." In ancient Hebrew psychology, the nose was thought to be the seat of anger. The word can mean "flaring nostrils." Synonyms used in the Old Testament for *anger* include *wrath* and *rage* (Esther 1:12), *overflowing rage* and *fury* (Amos 1:11), and *indignation* (Jeremiah 15:17). The emotion of anger can be the subject of Scripture even though the exact word is not present. Anger can be implied through words such as *revenge, cursing, jealousy, snorting, trembling, shouting, raving,* and *grinding of teeth.* Some parents use this definition with their children. When they see their child angry, they say, "How is your nose right now? Are your nostrils flaring?"

Several words are used for anger in the New Testament. It is important to note the distinction between these words. Many people have concluded that Scripture contradicts itself because in one verse we are taught not to be angry, and in another we are admonished to "be angry and sin not." Which is correct and which should we follow? You need to know the distinction, because it might very well come up with your children.

One of the words used most often for anger in the New Testament means "a turbulent commotion" or "a boiling agitation of feelings." This type of anger blazes up into a sudden explosion. It is an outburst from inner indignation and is similar to a match which quickly ignites but then burns out rapidly. Explosive anger is mentioned 20 times in the New Testament in passages such as Ephesians 4:31 and Galatians 5:20. We *are* to control this type of anger. Often you will see it demonstrated in the tantrums of a child.

Another type of anger, mentioned only three times in the New Testament (and never in a positive sense), is *parogiomos.* One place where *parogiomos* is used is in Ephesians 4:26: "Do not ever let your wrath (your exasperation, your fury or indignation) last until the sun goes down." This is anger that has been provoked. It is characterized by irritation, exasperation, or embitterment. A child who exhibits this is an unhappy child.

The most common New Testament word for anger is *orge*. It is used 45 times and means a more settled and long-lasting attitude which is slower in its onset, but more enduring. It often includes revenge. This kind of anger is similar to coals on a barbecue slowly warming to red and then to white-hot, holding this temperature until the cooking is done. Children and teens commonly display this sulking, vengeful behavior.

There are two exceptions where this word is used and revenge is not included in its meaning. Mark 3:5 records Jesus as having looked upon the Pharisees with anger, and Ephesians 4:26 tells us to "be...angry and sin not" (KJV). This is where anger is legitimate. The word *angry* in these verses means an anger which is an abiding and settled habit of the mind and is aroused under certain conditions. There is no revenge. You are aware of this kind of anger and it is under control. When careful reasoning is present, anger such as this is proper. The Scriptures not only permit it but on some occasions demand it! Perhaps this sounds strange to those who have thought for years that anger is all wrong. The Word of God does state that *we are to be angry!*

Righteous Anger

There are three main characteristics of righteous anger. First, it must be controlled. It is not a heated, unrestrained passion. Even if the cause is legitimate and is directed at an injustice, uncontrolled anger can cause an error in judgment and increase the difficulty of the situation. The mind must be in control of the emotions so the ability to reason is not lost. Perhaps the way this is accomplished is related to the scriptural teaching in Proverbs 14:29 and 16:32 to be "slow to anger" (NASB). This type of anger is not a direct result of immediate frustration. How will you teach your child to be slow to anger?

Second, there must be no hatred, malice, or resentment. Anger that harbors a counterattack only complicates the situation. Perhaps our best example of how to respond is Jesus' reaction to the injustices delivered against Him.

> When He was reviled and insulted, He did not revile or offer insult in return; [when] He was abused and suffered, He made not threats [of vengeance]; but He trusted [Himself and everything] to Him Who judges fairly (1 Peter 2:23).
>
> Beloved, never avenge yourselves, but leave the way open for [God's] wrath; for it is written, Vengeance is Mine, I will repay (requite), says the Lord (Romans 12:19).

When a child blames another, it is a counterattack. It is so natural to want another child to get into trouble. Misery loves company.

The final characteristic of righteous anger is that its motivation is unselfish. When the motivation is selfish, pride and resentment are usually involved. Anger should be directed not at the wrong done to oneself, but at the injustice done to other people. I have seen children come to the aid of another child being picked on, which is an example of righteous anger.

The basic overall theme of Scripture concerning anger is that it will be a part of life. It is not to be denied, but to be controlled. There is the key: control. Certain types of anger are not healthy and should be put away. Anger should be aroused against definite injustices, but then dealt with properly.

What about the type of anger that your child experiences? What is it like? How would you classify it after reading the above definitions? Take a few moments right now and try to think of some examples of each of these types of anger in your child's life. (What about your life?) Write down the situation and circumstances and describe the results of this anger. Describe how you think your child felt at the time and what the reactions of other people to him or her were.

Anger can be constructive. It can be used for good purposes if it is expressed properly. When the energy from this emotion is constructively redirected, you benefit from it.

How Angry Is Your Child?

Child's Name _____

The following inventory covers the more common signs of anger in children. All children occasionally manifest these signs, but if several of them are persistent, or if your child evidences many of them, you may have a problem.

Rate each statement according to the following scale and enter the rating in the appropriate space:

  0 – My child never or rarely does this.
  1 – My child occasionally does this (no more than once a month).
  2 – My child often does this (once a week or so).
  3 – My child does this frequently (daily or several times a week).

_____1. My child blames other people for his or her troubles.

_____2. My child throws or breaks things whenever he or she feels frustrated or irritated.

_____3. Whenever my child gets angry, calming him or her down takes a lot of placating.

_____4. My child does not like change of any sort and becomes angry when change is forced on him or her.

_____5. My child changes the rules of games when playing with other children.

_____6. My child says spiteful or hateful things whenever he or she is thwarted.

_____7. My child is negative, deliberately slow, and resists doing what he or she is told to do to the point that discipline becomes a standoff.

_____8. My child seeks out arguments or reasons to become upset, even when everything is at peace.

_____9. My child ostracizes, scorns, and complains about other people.

_____10. My child loses control when he or she is angry and shows it with facial expressions or body language.

_____11. My child uses foul language whenever he or she gets angry.

_____12. When my child is learning something new, he or she easily becomes frustrated and wants to do something else.

_____13. My child is stubborn and refuses to do what he or she is told to do unless you use the right tone of voice or approach.

_____14. My child's friends do not like to play with him or her because he or she is such a bad sport.

_____15. My child gets into fights with other children and has great difficulty controlling his or her temper when teased.

_____ Total Score

Test Interpretation

0–5   Your child is remarkably free of anger and is not prone to frustration. If anything, he or she may be a little too passive, but do not try to change this!

6–10   Your child is showing a normal degree of anger and frustration, but a higher score (nearer 10) is more appropriate for younger children (under 6 or 7), and a lower score (nearer 6) is more appropriate for older children.

11–15   Your child is beginning to show an above-normal degree of anger response. A higher score is more appropriate for younger children. Some attention to your child's response may be needed.

16–20   Clearly your child has a problem with anger and should receive your attention.

More than 20   Your child has a serious problem with anger, especially if he or she is already of school age. Take immediate steps to help your child cope with his or her anger, and seek professional help, if necessary.[3]

2

Understanding Anger

How can anger be beneficial rather than destructive? In what ways can this unwelcome and potentially destructive emotion be considered a gift to be used? Many parents see it as a missile to be avoided at all costs. There are certain facts that help us to understand anger's positive potential.

God has anger, and because we were made in His image, we have anger, too. In itself, it is not an evil or a destructive emotion. Nor is it always dangerous. Unfortunately, many people confuse the emotion of anger with the way some people choose to *express* that emotion. Many confuse anger with aggression. Anger is not the same as aggression. Anger is an emotion, while aggression is an action.

When we do not understand our anger and allow it to get out of control, it can lead to aggressive behaviors that are sinful, dangerous, and even deadly. The emotion of anger itself is not the problem. Sometimes from a parent's perspective, that is hard to see. The real problem is the mismanagement and misunderstanding of the emotion. The issue is the emotional immaturity of the individual who allows himself or herself to be controlled by the anger energy. Children have to learn to defuse and control that energy.

We cannot always control when or how we experience anger. But with God's help, we can learn to control how we choose to interpret and express it. Because God has made your child a rational creature, he is free to choose how he will respond to the events around him. However, he needs to learn that he has more control than he gives himself credit for.

Anger: A Secondary Emotion

Anger is a warning sign. Think of it as a clue to underlying currents. Anger is designed to help a person detect potentially destructive attitudes.

Anger may be the first emotion your child is aware of, but it is rarely the first emotion he or she experiences in a particular situation. The emotions that most frequently precede anger are fear, hurt, or frustration. Not only are these emotions painful, but they also drain any of us of energy and make us feel vulnerable.

Your child, even at an early age, learned that anger can divert his attention from these more painful emotions. He thinks, *If I get angry, I can avoid or at least minimize my pain. Perhaps I can even influence or change the source of my anger.* It does not take a child long to learn that it is easier to feel anger than it is to feel pain. Anger provides an increase of energy and can decrease a child's sense of vulnerability. Remember this when you see your child angry.

Unfortunately, most adults never realize that anger, like depression, is simply a message we are sending to ourselves.

When we experience hurt such as rejection, criticism, or physical or emotional pain, a normal reaction is anger. We strike back and counterattack against the source of our pain. "Let's get 'em" is our cry.

According to psychiatrist David Viscott in his book *The Language of Feelings* (Simon & Schuster, 1990) behind most anger is hurt and sadness. Think about what is hurting your child instead of focusing on his anger, and you may hit pay dirt. People feel hurt when they lose their sense of being loved (or lose someone they love), when they suffer a loss of esteem or competence, or if life seems unfair or less in their control.

Every parent, indeed every adult, who has ever spent time with a child, has seen what happens when anger and sadness get confused. Probably the most familiar example is the tearful tantrum. Although tears may be flowing copiously, tantrums are not really about sadness. They are about anger, frustration, and even rage.

Although they often look alike, anger and sadness are really very different. Anger is a distancing emotion. It pushes people away. Sadness, on the other hand, is an affirmative emotion. It draws people near. Anger is either the expression of a lack of vulnerability or a denial of vulnerability. The loneliness and vulnerability of the bully are not hard to perceive just beneath the surface hostility and off-putting (distancing) behavior. Genuine sadness, on the other hand, requires a willingness to tolerate vulnerability from both sides of the relationship.

Anger and Emotional Accessibility

Angry kids are inaccessible kids. Who would want to get close to them?

Whenever we work with an angry, mean, threatening, or off-putting child or adolescent, the first thing we try to do is to convert the anger into sadness. If a child screams that he "hates" his brother and then adds, "Besides, he never plays with me!" we say how sad it is that his brother will not involve him in his games. If a child erupts into rage because his Lego creation will not hold together, we tell him that it is okay to be sad that he could not get it to stand up on its own.

Preschool teachers and day-care providers, whose environments tend to be much more active and emotion-filled than elementary school classrooms, have told us that they have been amazed how much they can lower the aggression-revenge index just by defining angry responses in terms of sadness. These workers have found that responding to a child's anger and desire to hurt back with an empathetic remark such as "It's so sad that your beautiful building was knocked down" can often calm the angry reaction, thereby heading off a retaliatory response. Over time, the child internalizes the adult's definition of the experience and changes his response style. A preschool classroom in which adults routinely redefine traditionally angry responses in terms of sadness and disappointment tends to be a calmer and less aggressive environment. Just as in the clinical setting, such an environment tends to be much more conducive to whatever educational or therapeutic work needs to be done.

Another cause of anger is frustration, which we will discuss later.

Fear also causes anger. When children learn they are afraid of something, they rarely act afraid, but instead become angry. For some reason, anger is more comfortable than fear. Perhaps it is because we are on the offensive rather than the defensive. When you are afraid and act in anger, you confuse people around you. Children are quick to learn this. When angry, they are not telling people what they are really feeling inside, so all that other people can do is respond to the children's anger. Unfortunately, in most cases anger brings about more anger.

When you are angry, ask yourself these questions: "Do I feel hurt? Am I experiencing frustration over something? What am I frustrated about? Am I afraid of something at this time?" Write these questions on a 3"x 5" card and carry it with you as a reminder.

Talk to your children about this. Teach them to ask these questions when they are angry. If you see your child angry, instead of becoming angry at his or her anger, you could ask, "Are you feeling hurt over something right now? Are you frustrated about a situation at this time? Are you in some way afraid?" You might confuse him at first with these questions, especially if he is used to an argument or a strong reaction. Be persistent. In time you will see a difference.

Family therapists Gary and Carrie Oliver have taught their three boys to do this. They said:

> It's natural for children to experience joy, surprise, delight, fear, hurt, frustration, disappointment, discouragement, depression, and anger. Teach them how to identify and name their emotions. Ask them what they are feeling. Help them develop a vocabulary for their emotional life. This makes it easier for them to understand their own emotional life as well as talk about it with you.
>
> Let your kids know that you are encouraged when they identify their anger. This suggests that they are growing in their understanding of their emotions. It indicates that they are learning how to deal with this powerful emotion in healthy ways.
>
> Carrie and I have worked with each one of our three sons to help them name their emotions. One evening when we had company, our son Matthew came up and asked if he could talk to me. I excused myself from a conversation, lowered myself so that we were eye-to-eye, and asked him what was up. He said, "Dad, I'm angry."
>
> My first response was, "Thanks, Matt, I appreciate you letting me know." But as I said it, I realized that what

I said might need a bit more clarification, so I added, "Matt, I'm glad that you know when you're angry and that you want to talk about it." His ability to identify and label his emotion made it easier to help him deal with a difficult situation. Now he could express his anger in a constructive way rather than in a destructive fashion.[1]

The Many Disguises of Anger

We do not always recognize anger because it crops up in ways other than a physical or verbal response. What are some of the most common disguises anger can take? When we begrudge, scorn, or insult other people, or when we feel annoyed, offended, bitter, fed up, or repulsed, we are probably experiencing a form of anger. Some people exhibit anger by becoming sarcastic, tense, or cross. This anger can result when they feel frustration, exasperation, or wrath. Anger can also manifest itself as criticism, silence, intimidation, hypochondria, numerous petty complaints, depression, gossip, and blame. Do you see any of these in your children or teens?

Even behaviors such as stubbornness, halfhearted efforts, forgetfulness, and laziness can be evidence of anger.

Have you ever seen any of the following from your child?

- *Joking*—They hide intentional painful remarks with humor or ridicule.
- *Acting confused*—They pretend they do not understand you.
- *Appearing tired*—They act tired to avoid contact with you or someone else, or they agree with everything. They make passive comments with a certain tone of voice like, "Sure…" "Whatever…" and so on.

- *Not hearing*—They pretend they did not hear what you said.
- *Being clumsy*—They "accidentally" break something on purpose.

We call these passive-aggressive responses. And if they are used on you, they are quite irritating!

When is the last time your child admitted he was angry? If he did, how did he feel? Ashamed or embarrassed? Most of us are not comfortable admitting we are angry. And if this has not been modeled for a child, how will he know how to do this?

Three Choices for Dealing with Anger

Once your child admits he is angry, how can he deal with it? What choices are available to him?

There are three basic ways to deal with anger.

One way is to repress it—to never admit you are angry and simply ignore its presence. This repression is often unconscious, but it is not healthy! Repressing anger is like placing a wastebasket full of paper in a closet and setting fire to it. The fire will either burn itself out or else set the whole house on fire. The energy produced by anger cannot be destroyed. It must be converted or directed into another channel.

One outlet for repressed anger is accidents. Perhaps you have seen children who are accident-prone. Unfortunately, their accidents may involve other people as well as themselves. A child who is angry may slam a door on his own hand or his sibling's.

Repressed anger can easily take its toll on the body by giving you a vicious headache. Your child's gastrointestinal system reacts adversely to repressed anger. He could experience difficulty in swallowing, nausea and vomiting, gastric ulcer, constipation, or diarrhea. The most common cause of ulcerative colitis is repressed anger. Repressed anger can affect the skin through itching and neurodermatitis. Respiratory disorders such as asthma can be affected, and the role of anger in coronary thrombosis is fairly well-accepted.

At some time and in some way, the ignored or buried emotion of anger will express itself—physically, psychologically, or spiritually.

A second way your child can handle anger is to suppress it. This is where he is aware of his anger but chooses to hold it in and not let other people know he is angry. In some situations this may be wise, but eventually the anger needs to be recognized and drained away in a healthy manner. A child who always stuffs anger away is a sad case. The effort of keeping it in is an incredible waste of energy.

Though their cheerful, smiling exteriors make it seem otherwise, stuffers are usually unhappy children. Some literally stuff themselves by eating enormous amounts of food.

Suppressing anger does have some merit, especially if it helps your child relax, cool down, and begin to act in a rational manner. The Word of God has something to say about this type of suppression:

> He who is slow to anger has great understanding, but he who is hasty of spirit exposes and exalts his folly (Proverbs 14:29).

> He who is slow to anger is better than the mighty, he who rules his [own] spirit than he who takes a city (Proverbs 16:32).

> Good sense makes a man restrain his anger, and it is his glory to overlook a transgression or an offense (Proverbs 19:11).

> A [self-confident] fool utters all his anger, but a wise man holds it back and stills it (Proverbs 29:11).

This last passage means that the person does not give unbridled license to his anger but sort of hushes it up and puts it in the background. It also means that anger is overcome.

> I [Nehemiah] was very angry when I heard their cry
> and these words. I thought it over and then rebuked
> the nobles and officials (Nehemiah 5:6-7).

One version translates this last verse as "I consulted with myself."

A child or adult who practices self-control will find that his anger level actually decreases. He will not become as angry as if he were to simply cut loose with his first reaction. A calm consideration of the anger cause and the possible results will help a person handle the situation properly.

Expressing anger is a third way to handle it. Children are usually pretty good at this. Some people think you should express exactly how you feel no matter what or who is involved. They feel it is psychologically healthy and even necessary in order to live a balanced life. How wrong they are!

There are many different ways to express anger. The worst is to react with violent passion—yelling, harsh words, and swearing, and all with tremendous emotion. Have you ever heard this from your child?

The way your child expresses anger is a form of communication, and the more successful he is in communicating in a certain way, the greater the possibility he will continue that pattern. If he has been reinforced for being angry (has gotten what he wanted), then he will most likely continue to use his anger for manipulation.

The expression of anger does bring results. However, research shows that "letting out or fully expressing" your anger in a "cathartic way" does not reduce your frustration, but often leaves you more uptight instead. And angry outbursts invite retaliation. Just ask children and teens. They certainly know about this.

When a child expresses anger, it means he is more likely to do it again in the same way. He may let it out, but it does not stay out. When you express anger, you are not purging yourself of it but actually practicing it. Letting it all out may actually let it all back in. It moves you further from other people rather than drawing you closer.[2]

This can bring results, but not the kind you want. If you are allowed the freedom to react in this way, shouldn't the other person have the freedom to react to you in the same way? That puts another twist on it, doesn't it?

A child can also drain the energy of his anger by riding his bike around the block, digging in the garden for an hour, mowing the lawn, or writing a letter. Some of us are doers—actions seem to help. These solutions work if the child's mind is not going over angry thoughts during the process.

What doers need to keep in mind is that while riding their bike around the block, digging in the garden for an hour, mowing the lawn, or writing a letter may make them feel better, these activities are seldom directly related to the source of the anger.

Everyone (children and adults) is probably a doer some of the time. But if his only way of handling anger is to escape into physical activity, your child needs to ask himself the following questions from time to time: "At whom am I angry and why? How can I change things and feel better?"

Let's move on and explore more options to help a child with anger.

3
Your Child's Anger

Children grow up learning all kinds of myths about anger. Who do they learn it from? That's right: us. Adults!

Take a look at the following myths. You have probably heard these from your children, or perhaps you even believe them.

Myth #1: Anger is caused by other people. It could be another person—what they said or did, or it could be caused by a situation or an event.

This myth is not true. We may not like what happens outside of us, but we are responsible for the cause of our anger and what we do with it. Our children can learn this if they see us managing anger well. If we do not take responsibility for our anger, our anger begins to control and manage us.

Myth #2: Anger works, to get you what you want. It gets the attention of other people and it keeps them from controlling you.

The truth is, anger may *seem* to get you what you want right away, but in the long run it does not. Other people will either respond with anger or go away. It pushes people away. You lose friends, and you get a reputation that is hard to get rid of.

Myth #3: You feel better after you cut loose and express your anger. It does help to let it out, but only in ways that will not damage you and other people. Holding anger in and letting it pile up can be just as damaging.

There is a better way: Turn the anger down. Someone said there are three ways to handle anger. It is like a pot on a stove. You can put a lid on the pot or let it boil over. The third and best choice is to turn the heat down. How? Change what you are saying to yourself about other people or the situation. Our self-talk and beliefs can control our anger like the knob on a stove controls the temperature.

Another step to take in turning anger down is doing with yourself what you do with a boiling pot on the stove. Remove the pot and it begins to cool down. It helps to remove yourself from an upsetting situation that is feeding your anger.[1]

The Stages of Your Child's Anger

Is there a progression in the development of anger? Yes. It has been suggested by Dr. Tim Murphy that there are four stages of anger, and they are linked together. The first is the buildup. When an army is about to go to war, there is a tremendous buildup of resources and supplies. Children do the same, only they accumulate memories of hurts, frustrations, conflicts, and stress.

This buildup is like stacking up a pile of dynamite. Each stick represents some painful experience stored in his or her memory bank. Each has a fuse that can be shortened by being tired, hungry, sick, or having a bad day.[2] Dr. Murphy describes it this way:

> Our reactions to the present are influenced by the experiences of our past. Each time the stresses build in an angry child, that child comes closer to exploding. Experiences, learned attitudes, past reactions, and physical stresses all combine in the buildup stage. If these four factors have left the child angry at the world,

then you can expect to see a huge explosion when the
anger ignites.[3]

Does this sound like any child in your house? If so, what can
you do? Well, your goal is to prevent another outburst, if at all
possible, while at the same time you teach new ways of
responding. Help your child avoid painful and frustrating situations, while showing new and better ways of thinking about the
problem, as well as new responses and problem-solving skills.
Often children want to talk about the problem rather than the
solution. That is where you come in. Guide their thinking to new
solutions. Just asking, "What are three other ways to think about
what just happened?" can make a difference.

Many raging forest fires begin because of the smallest spark.
Thousands of acres are burned by something that began so small.
Anger can rise because of a spark. It can come from a sibling's
look, a word, a disappointment, or a thought. The spark—the
second stage of anger—could ignite a rage or a sullen look.

Sparks often come from an accelerated list of hurts and slights.
A child can reach into his or her history, distort the facts, and then
react. The problem is not really the spark. The problem is the
buildup that gives a spark its opportunity to be used. When a spark
falls into dry brush in a forest, the best way to prevent a major
blaze is to put out the spark before it can do its work. As a parent,
your task during the spark stage is to defuse the problem.

Children are predictable. Study your child. Make a list of his
or her sparks. Recognize these and act to prevent a firestorm. You
can listen in a calm manner, distract the child, suggest he or she
rethink what has happened, or ask the child to clarify for you what
the rules are, rather than you restating them.[4]

The third stage is what every parent dreads: the "volcanic
eruption." It is a stage you will not forget when those sticks of

dynamite end up in an explosion. Sometimes it is so intense that feelings are hurt and things may get broken. This is also the stage that causes you to lose *your* cool. You may have had some peaceful solutions in mind, but they just went out the window. A few of the angry child's expressions of anger may be acceptable, but most are not. Insults, put-downs, and sarcasm are common. Unfortunately, so is grabbing, hitting, kicking, throwing, and threats. The eruption can happen anywhere: at home, in the car, at the store, or at school. This is not a behavior in search of a solution, but an effort to dominate, punish, or even hurt.

What can you do? One author suggests your role is like being on the bomb squad. You try to defuse the bomb and minimize the effects or casualties. It is not easy. The problem is similar to what is described in Proverbs 22:24-25 (NIV), "Do not make friends with a hot-tempered man, do not associate with one easily angered, or you may learn his ways and get yourself ensnared."

You do not want to become like the angry person, but it is easy to get caught up in someone's anger. Why? You do not *think* your child should act like this, you do not *want* your child to act like this and, by golly, you *will not allow* this. Well…the reality is your child is already angry. Try thinking this way: "You know, I don't want my child behaving like this, but right at the moment he is. I can handle this. It's not the end of the world. In fact, I give him permission to do this right now. In time, we'll learn something new." When in your heart and mind you give him permission to be the way he is, your stress level goes down and you feel more in control. It works.

And when you engage your child, do the following:

- Do not model anger.
- Sit down and watch without saying anything.

- You could videotape the episode and then discuss it together at a later time.

- Hold to the rules you have established. You do not negotiate with terrorists or angry children. If you have not done so already, put all rules in writing. Stay out of arguments. Everyone loses.

- Repeat out loud what you think is occurring. If your child was hurt, let him experience hurt. If your child was afraid, let him experience fear. If your child was frustrated, let him experience frustration.

Probably the most overlooked but most important stage is the aftermath. This is the problem-solving stage. This is the time to discuss both original issues that generated the outburst and new ones brought about by the anger. In addition, you need to address the hurt feelings generated by the anger. The big questions to ask are, "What did we learn through this experience?" and "What can we do differently the next time?"

Some parents live in denial of their child's anger. They are afraid to confront the anger, hoping it will not erupt again. It will. For my job, I am involved in conducting debriefings when there has been a tragedy such as a robbery, accident, death, or any kind of trauma. We talk about the incident: what actually happened, what everyone thought at the time, and what they experienced or felt. We talk about the personal impact and how each person's life has changed.

Perhaps your child or teen would benefit from such a debriefing. They could learn what fed their anger, what they said to themselves about the event, what other feelings were there along with the angry ones. It may help them to spend time thinking about and writing answers to the following: "Is your anger getting you what you want? If not, there has got to be a better way to respond. What do you think you could do differently?" If your child gives cop-out answers to the last question, such as "Nothing," or "I don't know," respond with, "I think you're smart enough to come up with a better solution that that. Bring it with you to the next meal, and we'll talk about it then."

Angry outbursts carry a message: Something went wrong. As a parent, you need to function as a guide to get your child back on the trail to a new and better way.[5]

Now let's illustrate some anger situations and possible ways of responding. Let's listen in on a typical conversation that feeds anger.

> "No, Kathy, you can't go to the movies today."
>
> "That's not fair! Marcia's going. I hate your stupid rules."
>
> "Kathy, that's a bad attitude. After all the things I have let you do, the least you could do is stop arguing with me."
>
> "It isn't fair! All the other kids get to go. Michael gets to do more than me."
>
> "I let you go to lots of things this week. Don't give me all that stuff about I don't let you do anything. Don't you remember the other day?"
>
> "But I want to go today. You don't even care!"
>
> "I do care. How could you say that? All I ever do is cart you around from one place to another. How can you say I don't care? Now straighten up your attitude, or you aren't going anywhere for a week!"
>
> Kathy glares at her mother and then slams the door. There is anger here on both sides.

Let's replay the conversation and see if we get different results.

"No, Kathy, you can't go to the movies today. You have to do your chores first."

"That's not fair! Marcia's going. I hate your stupid rules."

"I know. It's frustrating when you don't get to go to the movies again."

"But I want to go today. You don't even care!"

"I know you're frustrated and angry. It's tough to have to work before you have fun. I feel that way, too."

"I hate living here! I don't ever get to do anything."

"I know. It's hard to miss the movies when you really want to go."

"Well, if you know so much, then let me go."

"I know you want to go. It's tough, but no."

"But if I miss this one, there won't be another sneak preview this summer."

"That's sad. It's a long time till next summer. I can see why you hate missing it so much."

Finally the child gets bored with not getting anywhere, either with moving the limit or frustrating the parent, and she gives up. She learns to accept reality.[6] Who responded differently here? How could you handle this?

Here's an example of 11-year-old Billy's challenge and anger:

"Mom, I'm going down to Joey's to play hockey. See ya later."

"No, Billy. You can't go. It's time to do your homework."

"Come on, Mom! Everyone's going. I can do my homework later."

"Billy, I understand you want to go, but we agreed that if you went swimming, you would work on your homework before dinner."

"Yeah, but I could do it after dinner."

"An agreement is an agreement. I don't want to talk about it anymore."

"You're just stupid. You don't understand anything. You're a big, fat, stupid."

If this sounds familiar, do not fret. Normal children naturally hate rules when you first set them. Your test is, What are you going to do when the child expresses anger and, in this case, disrespect? It is normal for disrespect to occur, but it is not normal for it to continue. The cure is empathy and correction, then consequences. What could his mother say at this point? Here are some ideas:

"Billy, I understand that you're really disappointed, but that's not the way to talk to me. Calling me 'stupid' is not okay. It hurts my feelings. It is okay to be sad or mad, but I won't allow name-calling. Let's talk about your feeling sad or mad."

"Billy, I understand you're upset. But when you call me stupid, how do you think that makes me feel?" (Wait for an answer so he has to think about how another person feels). "How do you feel when people call you names? Would you like to be treated that way?"

"Billy, I hear that you're ticked, and when you talk to me more respectfully, I'll be glad to listen. I won't listen to people who call me stupid. If you are upset about something, tell me in a different way."

"Billy, please think about what you just said and say it better."[7]

In the book *Setting Limits* by Robert MacKenzie, a cooldown technique is suggested. It is an excellent way to regain self-control.

Cooling down may not always be easy to do, especially if your emotions have begun to rise, but with preplanning, application of Scripture, prayer, and lots of practice, it will work. Memorizing and posting the following Scriptures will help a cooldown come more easily:

> But now put away and rid yourselves [completely] of all these things: anger, rage, bad feeling toward others, curses and slander, and foulmouthed abuse and shameful utterances from your lips! (Colossians 3:8).

> The terror of a king is as the roaring of a lion; whoever provokes him to anger or angers himself against him sins against his own life (Proverbs 20:2).

> A hot-tempered man stirs up strife, but he who is slow to anger appeases contention (Proverbs 15:18).

> He who is slow to anger is better than the mighty, he who rules his [own] spirit than he who takes a city (Proverbs 16:32).

> Make no friendships with a man given to anger, and with a wrathful man do not associate, lest you learn his ways and get yourself into a snare (Proverbs 22:24-25).

> When angry, do not sin; do not ever let your wrath (your exasperation, your fury or indignation) last until the sun goes down (Ephesians 4:26).

There are three ways to implement the cooldown approach with your child. If you both are upset, you could say, "It seems like we both need to calm down. Let's take a five-minute breather. I'll meet you in your room, and let's both think about how we could talk to one another in a different way." Be sure to use a timer.

If only your child is angry, you could say, "I can see you're angry. Let's take a five-minute time-out to cool down. You can be in your room or the living room. Which do you choose?"

If you are the one getting angry, you could say, "I'm angry right now, and I don't want to be. I want to calm down. I'll be in the other room for a while, and when I'm calm, we'll talk."[8]

Setting limits and rules for children can be the spark that ignites anger for many of them. Setting limits involves giving choices. That is realistic, because life is full of choices. Some choices just happen, while others are created. The parent who gives his child choices, will have a child who is being groomed to be an adult. A child who is not forced to make choices will have more difficulty coping with life, as well as with anger. When you give your child choices, you activate his brain and also make it easier on yourself. I have talked with parents of three-year-olds, six-year-olds, and nine-year-olds who all had the same question: "How can we have less hassles with the kids? What I ask them to do is simple, everyday stuff. There's got to be a better way to make a simple request, isn't there?"

There is. The authors of *Parenting with Love and Logic* have a very workable suggestion: Use "thinking words."

Children learn better from what they tell themselves than from what we tell them. They may do what we order them to do, but then their motivation for obedience comes from a voice other than their own: ours. Kids believe something that comes from inside their own heads. When they choose an option, they do the thinking, they make the choice, and the lesson sticks with them. That is why from early childhood on, parents must always be asking thinking-word questions: "Would you rather carry your coat or wear it?" "Would you rather put on your boots now or in the car?" "Would you rather play nicely in front of the television or be noisy in your room?"

We do not use fighting words: "You put that coat on now!" "Because *I* said put your boots on, that's why! It's snowing outside." "I'm trying to watch this football game. So *be quiet!*"[9] Did you hear the anger in these last statements?

Do you see the difference? Offering choices encourages cooperation without argument or hassle, as well as lessens the potential for anger.

The authors also make this suggestion: Instead of telling your child what to do, what you will not allow, or what you will not do for them, state the opposite.

Tell your child what you *will allow:* "Feel free to join us for dinner as soon as you've finished your chores."

Tell your child what you *will do:* "I'll be glad to help you with your homework as soon as you've cleared the table and rinsed everything."

Tell your child what you *will provide:* "You can eat what we're having, or you can see if you like the next meal better."[10]

Can you do this? Of course you can, with practice. Think of several incidents that you wish had gone better. Write down each incident the way you remember it. Now rewrite the incidents, giving your child a choice. Remember some of the phrases that have been suggested: "Feel free," "I'll be glad," and "You may." And be sure to use a soft, gentle tone of voice. Sometimes it is our tone that conveys our anger.

Yes, it will take some thought on your part.

Yes, it will take some time on your part.

And yes, this may surprise your child so he or she begins to think and comply. What do you have to lose by trying something different?

Whenever you have rules, you need consequences. They are the second part of setting limits. Consequences let a child know what is acceptable and what is not—and most importantly, who is in charge. They also hold a child responsible for his choices and behavior. And this is true of his anger as well.

A simple principle in theory, but one we do not always follow in our conversations is to request rather than command or demand. We might be amazed if we started to keep track of the number of orders we give to our children: "Do this, do that." "Put that away." "Don't leave the door open." "Stop doing that." "Go comb your hair." "Come to lunch." "Don't play with your food." "Get ready for bed now." "Don't stop." Ironically, we often repeat orders to make sure they are carried out, even though repetition weakens the response.

You can raise both the listening and compliance level of your child with one simple step: Ask. Instead of ordering, "Go clean your room," ask, "Would you please go and clean your room?" The word to use is *would*, not *could*. *Would* says, "I want you to," whereas *could* asks about competency. But no matter how you phrase it, note your tone.[11]

When you ask, avoid any long explanations. Keep it short. Have you ever felt your child watched too much TV or spent too much time playing video games? Probably. The following are examples of what some parents may say in situations like these, followed by some brief alternative questions to ask instead:

> "Kim, you've watched way too much TV today. That noise is getting to me. Turn it off and do something else with your time. Have you done your homework yet?"
>
> Instead say, "Would you please turn off the TV now and do something else?"

> "John, look at this room. There are clothes all over and dirty dishes—and the smell! Why can't you clean it up? I'm not going to pick up after you. Get a shovel and start cleaning."
>
> Instead, the following would suffice: "John, would you please clean your room? Thank you."

Here are 12 common negative expressions parents say to their children or teens. Read each one and decide if you have said this or something similar. There is a place for you to fill in when you used the expression, its result, and how you could rephrase the comment.

1. "You're not listening to me."
   The last time I said this was _____

   The result was _____

   The way in which I could rephrase this is _____

   _____

   _____

2. "Quit daydreaming and pay attention to me."
   The last time I said this was _____

   The result was _____

   The way in which I could rephrase this is _____

   _____

   _____

3. "Try to remember for once, will you?"
   The last time I said this was _____

   The result was _____

   The way in which I could rephrase this is _____

   _____

   _____

4. "I don't know what I'm going to do with you."
   The last time I said this was _____

The result was _____

The way in which I could rephrase this is _____

_____

_____

5. "There is no way you'll be able to do that."
   The last time I said this was _____

   The result was _____

   The way in which I could rephrase this is _____

   _____

   _____

6. "You didn't put your books (or toys, clothes, and so on) away."
   The last time I said this was _____

   The result was _____

   The way in which I could rephrase this is _____

   _____

   _____

7. "Your room is a total mess; it looks like a pigpen."
   The last time I said this was _____

   The result was _____

   The way in which I could rephrase this is _____

   _____

   _____

8. "Stop yelling in here. You're too loud."
   The last time I said this was _____

The result was _____

The way in which I could rephrase this is _____

_____

_____

9. "You forgot to say thank-you."
The last time I said this was _____

The result was _____

The way in which I could rephrase this is _____

_____

_____

10. "You left the door open again, and your clothes are on the floor."
The last time I said this was _____

The result was _____

The way in which I could rephrase this is _____

_____

_____

11. "Don't interrupt us when we're telling you something."
The last time I said this was _____

The result was _____

The way in which I could rephrase this is _____

_____

_____

12. Give an example of a common negative expression you usually say: _____

_____

The last time I said this was _____

The result was _____

The way in which I could rephrase this is _____

_____

_____

4
Anger Under Control

One of the best reasons for not allowing anger to get out of control is that it actually prevents a person from solving problems. You know this. Children need to learn there are better ways to respond. Anger is not a solution to frustration, but a reaction to frustration. If your child is persistently bugging you to take him or her to Disneyland, the solution is to talk about it.

If you, as the parent, do not like your working conditions, what can you do? You can either attempt to improve the working atmosphere, learn to live with an undesirable (but not intolerable) situation, or look for another job. Getting angry will not bring about positive, lasting improvements in which all parties are satisfied. If your child does not like his or her school, getting angry is not the solution.

One way of dealing with anger is to approach it from the perspective of frustration. If anger has been brought about by frustration, it will have a tendency to disappear if the frustration is removed. If your child is angry because a planned fishing trip was suddenly canceled, he will tend to quiet down if he is able to go on some other outing. If you are angry because your child is not responding to your attempts at discipline, your anger will sub-side when he begins behaving.

Remember this: The energy of anger does not have to be unleashed in a manner that will hurt or destroy. Instead, it can be used in a constructive manner to eliminate the frustration. If the original frustration cannot be eliminated, many people learn to accept substitute goals and thereby receive nearly as much, and sometimes even greater satisfaction.

Reacting with anger to frustration is like pouring gasoline on a fire that is already blazing. A chemical retardant would be far better. Proverbs 15:1 illustrates an appropriate response: "A soft answer turneth away wrath: but grievous words stir up anger" (KJV).

This verse does not say that the other person's anger will be turned away immediately, but in time it will happen. Remember, you will have to plan your verbal and nonverbal response to your child well in advance and even practice it if you expect it to happen. If you wait until you are in the heat of an altercation, you will not (and cannot because of physical changes) be able to change your old angry way of reacting. Visualizing and practicing the scriptural teaching in advance prepares you to make the proper response. You as a parent *will* be frustrated with your child. How you respond will teach your child how to respond to his or her own frustrations. Let's consider your frustration first.

So, why do *you* become angry at your family members when they do not respond to you? Why do you get angry at the kids when they do not pick up things in their room, mow the lawn, or dry the dishes properly? Anger expressed by yelling at a son who does not mow the lawn carefully does not teach him how to do it correctly. Angry words directed to a sloppy daughter do not teach her how to be neat. Step-by-step instruction (even if it has been given before) can help solve the problem.

Another result of anger is that you (yes, you the parent) become a carrier of a very infectious germ: anger itself. If you respond in anger, people around you can easily catch the germ. If you become angry at your spouse, do not be surprised if he or she responds in a like manner. You gave your husband or wife an example to follow. Your spouse is responsible for his or her own emotional responses, but you still modeled the response. Perhaps if you respond with a kind, but firm reply, your spouse will follow this example. And so will your child.

Reducing Your Frustration

I hear people in my office and in my seminars say to me again and again, "Norm, I don't want to talk in an angry way to others, especially my family, but something just comes over me and I let it rip! There's a limit to what I can take. I know I really love them, but sometimes I don't like them very much. I don't know what to do to change."

I usually respond with a question: "When you feel frustrated and angry with your family members, what do you focus on: how they react at what you said, or how you would like them to act?"

They usually reply, "Oh, I keep mulling over what I didn't like and my destructive comments. I relive it again and again and beat up on myself for hurting them."

"Do you realize that by rehearsing your failures you are programming yourself to repeat them?" I ask.

They respond with a puzzled look. But it is true. When you spend so much time thinking about what you should not have done, you reinforce the negative behavior. Furthermore, spending all your time and energy mentally rehashing your failures keeps you from formulating what you really *want* to do. Redirecting your time and energy toward a solution will make a big difference in how you communicate with anyone. Focus your attention on how you want to respond to your frustration and you *will* experience change!

Let's consider several steps you can take to reduce your frustration and to curb words that you do not want to express. This will help teach your child by example.

The first step is to find someone with whom you can share your concerns and develop an accountability relationship. Select someone who will be willing to pray with you and check up on you regularly to see how you are doing. If you are working through these steps as a couple, ask another couple to keep you accountable. We all need the support and assistance of other people.

You also need to be honest and accountable to yourself and others about changes you want to make. Take a sheet of paper and respond in writing to the following questions. Then share your responses with your prayer partner:

- How do you feel about becoming frustrated? Be specific. How do you feel about getting angry? There are some people who enjoy their frustration and anger. It gives them an adrenaline rush and a feeling of power. Does this description fit you in any way?

- When you are frustrated, do you want to be in control of your response or be spontaneous? In other words, do you want to decide what to do or just let your feelings take you where they want to go?

- If you want to stay in control, how much time and energy are you willing to spend to make this happen? For change to occur, the motivational level needs to remain both constant and high.

- When you are bothered by something that someone else does, how would you like to respond? What would you like to say at that time? Be specific.

There is a reason why God inspired men to write the Scriptures and why He preserved His words through the centuries for us: God's guidelines for life are best. Regardless of what you may have experienced or been taught in the past, God's plan works!

Write out each of the following verses from Proverbs on separate index cards:

> Reckless words pierce like a sword, but the tongue of the wise brings healing (12:18 NIV).

> A patient man has great understanding, but a quick-tempered man displays folly (14:29 NIV).

> Better a patient man than a warrior, a man who controls his temper than one who takes a city (16:32 NIV).

Add to your card file other Scriptures you discover that relate to frustration and anger. Read these verses aloud morning and evening for three weeks, and you will own them.

You will be able to change only if you plan to change. Your intentions may be good, but once the frustration-anger sequence kicks into gear, your ability to think clearly is limited.

Identify in advance what you want to say when you begin to feel frustrated. Be specific. Write out your responses and read them aloud to yourself and to your prayer partner. In my counseling office, I often have clients practice their new responses on me, and I attempt to respond as the other person might. By practicing on me, they are able to refine their statements, eliminate their anxiety or feelings of discomfort, and gain confidence for their new approach. Your spouse or prayer partner could assist you in this way.

Begin training yourself to delay your verbal and behavioral responses when you recognize that you are frustrated. The book of Proverbs repeatedly admonishes us to be *slow* to anger. You must slow down your responses if you want to change any habits of words you have cultivated over the years. When we allow frustration and anger to be expressed unhindered, they are like a runaway locomotive. You need to catch them before they gather momentum so you can switch tracks and steer your emotions in the right direction.

One helpful way to change direction is to use a trigger word. Whenever you feel frustration and anger rising within you, remind yourself to slow down and gain control by saying something to yourself like *Stop! Think! Control!* and so on. Those are words that will help you switch gears and put your new plan into action.

A quick tool to reduce frustration is to give your child permission to be a certain way or to do certain things. The permission-giving approach defuses your frustration and gives you time to implement a levelheaded plan.

Do not get me wrong. I am not suggesting that you emotionally give up and allow your child to do anything he wants to do. There are some behaviors which are highly detrimental to a child and require a firm and immediate "No!" But with everyday behaviors, which are more frustrating than dangerous, challenge yourself to quit fighting and go with the flow. By doing so, you may be able to skirt your child's defenses and solve the problem without wounding him by coming unglued.

Many parents are skeptical when I suggest the permission-giving strategy. However, they often come back after trying it and report amazing results. One mother said, "Norm, the first time I heard your suggestion, I thought you were crazy. But I tried it. I discovered that I was less frustrated. My posture was less rigid, and I was more relaxed as I dealt with my son. One day he said,

'Mom, you're doing something different. You're not getting so uptight, and you seem to be hearing what I say.' That was all the reinforcement I needed!"

Change Your Inner Conversation

Your inner conversation—also called self-talk—is where your frustrations are either tamed or inflamed. What you say to your children and how you behave toward them is determined by how you talk to yourself about their behaviors and responses. In fact, your most powerful emotions—anger, depression, guilt, worry— as well as your beliefs about yourself as a person and a parent, are initiated and fed by your inner conversation. Changing your inner conversation is essential to keeping your parenting frustrations from erupting into wounding words.

Just before leaving for his Saturday-morning golf game, Art asked his 11-year-old son to clean up his room and wash the family car. Jimmy said he would. But when Art returned home, Jimmy was nowhere to be seen. His room was only half-clean, and the car was still a mess. Let's listen in on Art's inner conversation as he surveys the scene:

> Where is that boy? He didn't follow my instructions. He's so lazy and inconsiderate. I give him everything, and he doesn't even have the courtesy to do a little work. He never follows through. Wait till I see him. And he always leaves without writing a note telling me where he's going. I'll ground that kid for a month!

You may argue that Art had the right to be frustrated and angry. Maybe so, maybe not. Regardless, Art was free to choose how he thought about the scene before him. And his inner conversation reveals that he chose to fuel his frustration with distorted thinking. He resorted to labeling, calling Jimmy lazy and inconsiderate.

Labeling encourages frustration because it perpetuates a negative view. You begin to look for behaviors in your child which reinforce the labels you have attached to him. You tend to overlook the positives and look for the worst.

Another evidence of Art's distorted thinking is magnification. Words like *never, always,* and *every* magnify occasional misbehaviors into lifetime habits. Magnifying the child's misbehavior only serves to intensify parental frustration.

Art's inner conversation was based on hasty, negative assumptions. Perhaps an emergency in the neighborhood called Jimmy away from his task. Perhaps an out-of-town relative arrived unexpectedly and took Jimmy to the mall for the afternoon. Perhaps a shut-in down the street called Jimmy to run an important errand. Maybe he left a note explaining his whereabouts, but Art was so busy thinking the worst that he did not look for it. You will save yourself a lot of frustration and anger if you learn to base your inner conversations on hard facts and positive assumptions.

God's Word has a lot to say about how we think. If you have difficulty with negative inner conversations, I suggest you write out the following Scriptures on index cards and begin reading them aloud to yourself every morning and evening: Isaiah 26:3; Romans 8:6-7; 2 Corinthians 10:5; 12:2; Ephesians 4:23; Philippians 4:6-9; 1 Peter 1:13. Your thoughts can change if you choose to change them.

Adopt a Hopeful Attitude

If you approach these steps thinking, "This will never work," you have set yourself up for failure. Instead, coach yourself to think, "I'm taking some positive steps toward resolving my frustration and anger. This will really make a difference in my relationship with my child. I know my communication with him will improve as I take these steps of growth."

To help you to develop a positive attitude, take a minute to list the advantages of being frustrated and the advantages of not being frustrated. Compare the two lists. Which results do you want? You are more likely to achieve these results by following the steps above.

A Record of Progress

Keep a record of your progress by maintaining a frustration diary in a small notebook. Keep your notebook handy at all times so you can write down your responses to your parenting frustrations. Share your entries with your spouse or prayer partner, but not with your children.

The purpose of this diary is twofold. First, it will help you arrest your frustrations as they arise so you can control them instead of allowing them to control you. Second, it will help you plan a healthy, controlled response to future frustrations.

Here's a pattern for your frustration-diary entries:

- The date and time the frustration occurred:
- The level of my frustration on a scale of 0 (none) to 10 (intense) was...
- My frustration was directed toward...
- Inside I felt...
- My inner conversation about my child and his behavior could be summarized as...
- My verbal response to my child was...

- Did I move from frustration to anger? If so, what was the intensity of my anger?
- How did my response this time improve from the previous frustration experience?
- What would I like to feel and say at the next incident of frustration?
- What improvement will I make at the next incident of frustration?

Here is an example of how one woman—30-year-old Janice, mother of two preschoolers—charted her progress in her frustration diary:

- The date and time the frustration occurred: *Wednesday, February 6, at 11:30 A.M., just before lunchtime.*
- The level of my frustration on a scale of 0 (none) to 10 (intense) was...*an 8!*
- My frustration was directed toward...*my five-year-old, Stacy.*
- Inside I felt...*really irritated. In fact, I was ready to go over and grab her.*
- My inner conversation about my child and her behavior could be summarized as: *That child is so stubborn. She doesn't listen to me. Her behavior is so selfish. I wonder how anyone can stand her when she's like that.*
- My verbal response to my child was: *"Stacy, you're impossible. You know you heard me. At times you are so bad!"*
- Did I move from frustration to anger? If so, what was the intensity of my anger? *You bet I did! I was upset, and my anger rose to about level 8 also.*

- How did my response this time improve from the previous frustration experience? *I'm not sure it did. It may have been louder. But I don't think it lasted as long this time, so I guess I could call that an improvement.*

- What would I like to feel and say at the next incident of frustration? *I don't want to feel irritated and angry. I guess I would like to talk to her in a firm, calm voice, but also get through to her.*

- What improvement will I make at the next incident of frustration? *I think I need to figure that out more in detail now. I'm going to memorize Proverbs 12:18; 14:29; and 16:32. Then I'm going to write out and practice exactly what I will say when Stacy doesn't mind me. I'm also going to discuss and role-play the situation with my prayer partner.*

  I'm going to use the "conscious delay principle." I will stop for a few seconds and remember what I want to say and do. In fact, in my mind I'm going to say, "It's all right for this to be happening. Most of her misbehavior isn't dangerous or life-threatening to her, and it's not the end of the world for me."

  Then I am going to go to Stacy, kneel down to her level, put my hand gently on her shoulder, look her in the eye, and in a calm voice ask, "What did I just tell you to do?"

  This approach may make a difference.

Janice's approach, carefully planned and written in her diary, did make a difference.

I hope you truly believe that you can change your responses to the frustrations you face. God believes you can. He is the One who can support you in your journey of change. Allow your spouse and your friends to help and support you also. Above all, believe that you can change and that your change will make a difference in your parent-child communication.

For Thought and Discussion

Share your responses to the following steps with your spouse, a trusted friend, or your study group.

On a scale of 0 (desperate improvement needed) to 10 (no improvement needed), rate your present success at implementing each of these steps to reducing parental frustration.

1. Be honest and accountable.

0   1   2   3   4   5   6   7   8   9   10

2. Internalize the guidelines from God's Word.

0   1   2   3   4   5   6   7   8   9   10

3. Plan your response to frustration in advance.

0   1   2   3   4   5   6   7   8   9   10

4. Learn to delay your responses.

0   1   2   3   4   5   6   7   8   9   10

5. Make room for your child's frustrating behavior.

0   1   2   3   4   5   6   7   8   9   10

6. Change your inner conversation.

0   1   2   3   4   5   6   7   8   9   10

7. Adopt a hopeful attitude.

0   1   2   3   4   5   6   7   8   9   10

Practice using the frustration diary by filling in the sample page below as it relates to the last incident of frustration you remember experiencing with your child.

- The date and time the frustration occurred:
- The level of my frustration on a scale of 0 (none) to 10 (intense) was…
- My frustration was directed toward…
- Inside I felt…
- My inner conversation about my child and his behavior could be summarized as…
- My verbal response to my child was…
- Did I move from frustration to anger? If so, what was the intensity of my anger?
- How did my response this time improve from the previous frustration experience?
- What would I like to feel and say at the next incident of frustration?
- What improvement will I make at the next incident of frustration?

What About Other People's Anger?

It is important for you to clarify in your own mind why you want to reduce the amount of anger in other people such as your children. You may simply find anger distasteful, or you could be afraid that it might get out of hand. You might feel that it prolongs disagreements rather than resolves them. Know why you're uncomfortable with your children's anger, and at a calm time explain your position to them.

Second, as you respond to your children's anger, remember that their anger is not the true emotion. Regardless of how intense and destructive their anger is, it is still an expression of their fear, hurt, or frustration. Unfortunately, the anger camouflages this and does not clearly identify the problem for you. If you can give them permission in your own heart and mind to be angry, it will be easier for you not to respond in anger yourself. Then you can concentrate on the real issue between the two of you, as well as the underlying cause of the anger. When you can learn to avoid responding to their anger with your own, you have taken a giant step forward.

There are several ways in which you can help to defuse the anger of other people. One way is for you to heed a "prior agreement." Sometimes parents and children (or couples) work out an agreement or covenant on how they will act during their disagreements.

Zones of Anger

Some people like to use a stress-reduction card to measure their excitement. A small chemically treated square, sensitive to heat and moisture, measures a person's level of stress. You place your thumb on the square for ten seconds, and your level of stress will turn the square either black, red, green, or blue, depending upon how tense or excited you are. The green and blue color zones reflect calm, with little or no stress.[1] This could be a game for the kids. These squares can be purchased on the Internet.

There are proper zones to stay in with anger as well. Family members often move out of the green or blue zone of anger into a red zone. The green or blue zones show you are being objective and logical. The red zone shows you are feeling intense, irrational anger. In between, in what is called a yellow zone, you feel anger toward the other person but are able to exert control over your thoughts and actions. You can still let the other person know that you are angry and need to express it, but not at the expense of the relationship.

When a person moves from the yellow to the red zone, all the symptoms of the yellow zone have been intensified. This "red" anger is characterized by attacking the person rather than the problem, being irrational, hurling accusations, and demeaning the other person's character. You believe the other person deserves everything you are dishing out. This is where lasting damage can occur. The blue zone is characterized by calm presentations and listening.[2]

It is possible to learn to identify which zone you are in, let the other person know, and also identify which zone you are working toward. As one teen said, "I'm hovering between the yellow and red, and I don't like it either. I want to get rid of how I'm feeling and get into the blue zone. Please listen to me, Dad."

Some parents and kids make little flags of each color and pin them up in a predesignated spot to denote the level of their anger. Some have made this a family project in which everyone has his or her own set of flags. Each person keeps his set of flags with him during a discussion or disagreement and holds the appropriate one to let other family members know his anger level. When a person has chosen to use the flags to convey a message about his anger, he is demonstrating some control over his emotions.

Talk or Write?

In this process of defusing yourself and the other person, it may be helpful to ask, "What would be best for us right now: to talk about our anger, or to write it out?" For those people who have difficulty verbalizing, writing may help them release feelings that they tend to carry inside. And for the highly verbal, writing may keep them from saying too much at the wrong time. In addition, writing often helps people to see the issues more clearly than talking about them. You can decide whether to reveal what you have written or keep it just for your own expression. This will only work with your child if he can write.

When you write, you can simply list your feelings and identify the cause of your anger. You can write what you would never say directly to your child, or you can write an angry (unmailed) letter, which you might read aloud in an empty room. Then burn or destroy the letter. Once the letter is destroyed, go back to your child and discuss the problem. Remember, anger patterns are learned, and so are solutions.

5

How to Help Your Child Deal with Anger

Let's recap what you have (hopefully) learned by now to help your child deal with anger.

- First, the Word of God has much to say about anger and presents it in a balanced way.
- Anger is a secondary emotion.
- Most anger is caused by fear, hurt, or frustration.
- Anger is often disguised.
- Three ways to deal with anger include: repress it, suppress it, or express it. The best way is to turn the anger down. One way to do this is by changing what we say to ourselves.
- There are usually four stages in the progression of your child's anger.
- How you say something and what you say affect your anger and your child's response.
- Model how you would like your child to respond.

Where do you go from here? Well, that is what this chapter is about. It is a resource chapter. You may even feel overwhelmed with all the practical suggestions you are going to encounter. They have been gleaned from many different sources. You may not use them all, but you will have a good selection. One idea may work best with one child, and a different one with another. But you will have some suggestions that have worked for many parents.

The first suggestion is, Watch what you say. Avoid saying the following "parent phrases":

- "I don't know why you're so angry. That doesn't seem like a big issue."
- "Here's what I think you should do…"
- "Quit acting like a baby."
- "Can we talk later? I'm busy now."
- "You'll just have to deal with it as best you can."
- "I'd have punched his/her lights out."
- "I don't want to hear that expression again."
- "What do you want now? Can't you see I'm busy?"
- "Can't you ever stay out of trouble?"
- "Don't lose your temper with me! You're grounded!"

Here are some others words and phrases to avoid with your child:

- "Be quiet."
- "How can you…"
- "I'm busy."
- "It's nothing."
- "Let me tell you…"
- "Never…"
- "Not again."
- *revenge*
- *stupid*
- "Wait until I tell your…"

- "You're in trouble."
- "You're silly."[1]

Have you ever said the following?

> "Don't you talk to me in that tone of voice!" Probably. Did it work? Probably not. And what was your tone like? If only we had a tape recorder. Or have you said, "Don't you dare use that tone of voice (or slam the door, kick the cat, etc.)!"
>
> "Oh, do you know how that makes me feel? That hurt me so much I could cry." Is your child concerned about your feelings at this time? Probably not. He is into his own.
>
> "I will not talk to you when you're like this." What if your child or teen does not want you to talk to them? You have just fallen into their plan.[2]

Your goal is to help your child or teen to *manage* her anger. How? Focus on the positive. You could relate this present experience to other times she has been angry and how she handled it in a positive way. You could share some of the following:

- "I can see why you're so angry. I didn't like those situations either. But now you're at a place where you can have a choice."
- "The last time you were this angry, do you remember what you did to get over it? Tell me about it. You did something really positive. Can you remember?"
- "This is what I do when I'm angry. It may work for you."
- "Let's take this anger apart, look at what caused it, and then figure out what you can do about it."
- "It helps to talk when you're angry. Think about this for a while and then tell me what you would like to do. Maybe I can help you."

Once the two of you understand the anger, you can help channel it into something positive. Ask questions to help your child problem-solve:

- "What do you think you can do so it doesn't happen again?"
- "Which of these things would work best for you?"
- "If this happened to someone else, what advice would you give that person?"
- "When something like this happens, what can you control and what can't you control? How can you handle what you can't control?"
- "Have you ever done something that upset another person? What did you learn from that experience? What would you do and not do again?"[3]

What can you say to teach your preschooler and elementary-age child about anger? You can read the following to them, dress up and act it out, or tape it. Some creative parents have made a video of this, with their children dramatizing the parts.

> OK. It's time to fess up. Did you get angry today? Yes? No? What about yesterday? Well, what about this week? Who knew you were angry? Well, you probably did. What about your mom or dad? Your friend? The dog or cat? Someone did. And that's better than trying to fool other people.
>
> Your anger will come out one way or another. It could be a pout or a shout. It could be a glare or a stare. Did you know some kids or even adults won't admit they're angry? That's right. They won't. They even say, "Oh, no. Not me. Angry? Never." But their face turns red, their eyes get big, their stomach hurts, and their voice gets loud. But they're not angry. Or are they? Your body will tell you and it will tell other people you're

angry. So why not admit it? After all, there is one person who always knows what we're thinking and feeling. God knows. In Psalms it says, "When far away you know my every thought....You know what I am going to say before I even say it" (Psalm 139:2,4 TLB). God created you with the ability to get angry. It's true. And He wants you to use it in the right way.

Some people talk about anger as a monster. Well, it's not always a monster. But sometimes your mind and body act in "monstrous" ways.

Your brain gets angry. It races and races with terrible thoughts. (Can you think of one?)

You feel like yelling, shouting, screaming, or even cursing. (Can you think of a time?)

You grit your teeth (and sometimes they hurt. Ouch!).

You look mean at people—you scowl or frown or even show your teeth. (When was the last time this happened?)

You make your hands into fists. (Does this mean you want to hit? Uh-huh.)

Your heart starts pounding. It goes faster and louder. (That's normal.)

Your stomach feels like it's turning over and over and gurgles and even hurts. It's like there's a volcano in your tummy. (Tell me a time that happened.)[4]

What do your feet want to do? Stomp? Kick?

What do you want to do with your anger? Do you want it to stay around and smell up your life like a pair of stinky, old socks? Or do you want to get rid of it? You have a choice. (If you hear an "I don't know," take the next step.)

Let's look at the results of being angry and not being angry. What do you think?

Being angry	Not being angry
1.	1.
2.	2.
3.	3.
4.	4.
5.	5.

How can you tell if you're angry? Listen to your mind and your body.

Remember what we just talked about? That's how to tell if you're getting angry. What goes on in your mind and body tells you what's going on with your emotions.

And when we get angry, it would help if we had an anger thermometer that could let us (and other people) know just how angry we are. Here's one. Perhaps we could use this scale for ourselves and to help other people know where we are:

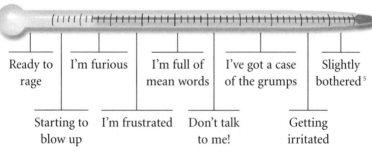

Ready to rage	I'm furious	I'm full of mean words	I've got a case of the grumps	Slightly bothered[5]

Starting to blow up	I'm frustrated	Don't talk to me!	Getting irritated

Yes, we all get angry. You can let your anger control you, or you can control your anger. How do you think you could control your anger? Let's list five ways:

1. When you are angry, pick at least four of the words from this list to describe your anger:

mad	furious	riled-up
cranky	burned-up	hot
annoyed	crabby	grumpy
snarly	ornery	mean
bitter	raging	resentful
ticked-off	bugged	out-of-control

2. Now discover what is causing your anger. It is not anyone else. Other people do not make us angry. We make ourselves angry. Remember the three big causes for anger? They are frustration, fear, and hurt.

3. Ask yourself, "What caused my anger?" Write your answers below.

    A.

    B.

    C.

4. Which of the following Scriptures would help you when anger hits?

    A person who quickly gets angry causes trouble (Proverbs 15:18 NCV).

Patience is better than strength. Controlling your temper is better than capturing a city (Proverbs 16:32 NCV).

What Can You Do When Your Child Is Angry at You?

1. Do not retaliate. (Joining in the child's anger will wind her/him up even more. It will also teach her/him poor ways of resolving conflict).

2. Model the behavior you want a child to learn. If you hit, your child learns to hit. If you get out of control, your child may learn to fear her/his own anger (or teachers, or school, or men).

3. Let your child know you understand how she/he is feeling: "I can see how angry you are," or "It seems like you're really mad about that."

4. Leave explaining another point of view until the anger has been expressed and acknowledged.

5. Ask what your child would like to do to improve things.

6. Acknowledge what your child says. Reaffirm the feelings, and then help look at the options, such as, "What might happen if you did that?"

7. Do not force children into apologizing when they do not feel sorry. You may be forcing them to bury their anger and be teaching them to be hypocritical.

If Two Children Are Angry with Each Other

1. Reflect what you see happening: "*I see two children fighting over a ball.*"

2. Separate the children if need be for safety's sake. Say, "*Someone might get hurt.*"

3. Give them both a way of venting their anger: *"When you've got your anger out, we'll talk about it. You run to the front fence, you run to the back fence and come back to me."*

4. Find out what they each need: *"It looks like you need something to play with."*

5. Find out what they are afraid of: *"Are you worried you won't get a turn if you give him the ball?"*

6. Ask for some solutions.

7. Give a child a sheet of paper and say, *"It seems that you're furious. Draw me a picture and show me how angry you are."* Acknowledge the picture. *"I can see you're really mad. What do you want to do with this picture? How are you feeling right now? What might you do the next time you feel as angry as that?"*

If a child has hurt another, look the offender in the eye and say firmly, *"We don't hit. It hurts."* Attend to the victim and reflect their feelings. *"You were kicked on the leg. I bet that hurts. Draw me a picture and show me how you feel."*[6]

If you are working together as a family, have every person draw what each of you looks like when angry. Draw your faces in the circles below. More circles can be added, if needed.

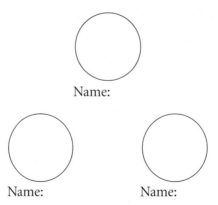

Name:

Name:

Name:

Ask everyone to write down the thought that helped to create the anger next to his or her angry face:

The thought that made me angry was _____

_____

_____

What do you need to do to control your anger?

What will you do the next time you're angry?

How to Talk to Your Child About Anger

Empathizing is usually the best bet for openers. Calmly reporting your observations or your reaction can also help:

- "When you're angry like that, I know you must be sad about something. Tell me what happened."
- "It hurt your feelings when your brother knocked your new bike over on purpose."
- "If you're angry, you must have a pretty good reason. Please tell me what it is."
- "When you're yelling, it is hard for me to concentrate. Please lower your voice."
- "You just slammed the door. That tells me you're hurt about something. I would like you to tell me what's wrong."
- "I remember saying that to my father when I was a kid. I felt a lot better when we talked about it."
- "I can't force you to talk about it if you don't want to. I just hope you change your mind, because talking usually helps. Besides, I hate to see you feeling so bad."

When your child is calmer, it is a good idea for each of you to sit while talking. Standing up increases the chances of another angry outburst or someone walking away prematurely.

- "Jimmy, even though you feel hurt and angry, I liked it much better when you talked more calmly. I was able to listen and really hear you. Let's do this again."
- "Guess what! That was helpful. You were able to speak more softly and with less anger. I know, it isn't always easy to do that when you're upset, but you did it."

Gary and Carrie Oliver have suggested:

> Without a plan to deal with anger, we are more likely to say things that hurt rather than heal—more likely to do things we will regret. One way to help a child choose healthy responses to anger is to remind the child of what has or hasn't worked in the past.
>
> Take this common scenario, for instance. Timmy storms into the house, slams the front door, stomps up the stairs to his bedroom, and slams *that* door, too. So far, fairly predictable eight-year-old angry male behavior. His mother goes to his room and asks what's wrong.
>
> "Aaron said he's not going to invite me to his birthday party, and I invited him to mine. I hate him, and I never want to see him again."
>
> Karen waits for a moment, just in case Timmy wants to add anything, before saying, "Sounds like you're really hurt by what Aaron said. I know four different ways you can handle this hurt, and some of them may work. If you want to hear them, let me know." She gives her fuming boy a hug, then leaves the room.
>
> A few minutes later Timmy appears at the door to his mom's home office. "So, what are they?" he asks.

"Do you really want to know?"

Timmy mumbles, "Yes."

"Well," she said, "here they are. Some of them might be better than others, but you can decide. One: I could set the timer for 15 minutes and go into my room and kick and scream and pound on the floor until the timer goes off. Two: I could call three of my friends and tell them what a terrible, awful, horrible person Aaron is. Three: I could write a letter to God and tell him how sad and hurt I am, and then read the letter to a friend. Four: I could tell my mom how sad and hurt I am, and then maybe we could pray and talk about how I can choose to respond."

Timmy opts for number four, and he and his mom end up having a profitable discussion about his decision in the end.[7]

Gary and Carrie also suggest:

Don't ever try to handle your son's anger for him. It's *his* anger, and he has to deal with it. But you *can* help. After asking his older brother several times to stop teasing him, our seven-year old took off his snow boot and threw it at his nemesis. The boot bounced off Nathan's head, prompting him to run down the stairs yelling, "Matt hit me with his boot."

What was the best way to respond? We certainly could have been upset at both of them, or told them, "Now you really shouldn't get mad at each other," or "There's no excuse for that kind of behavior." Our dilemma was this: How do we honor the feelings and concerns of both boys and yet help them deal with the real issue? The situation had occurred before, and so we were a bit better prepared to help them take responsibility for their own problem and thereby learn something valuable from this incident.

"It's probably frustrating to be teased," said Carrie, "and I know it hurts to have a boot bounce off your head. But Nathan, do you know what it feels like to be teased? You've been teased before—how do you like it? And, Matt, did Nathan's teasing make it right for you to throw your boot at him? What could you have done besides flinging your boot at him?

"So I'm giving you this opportunity to go to your room and discuss the choices you have. What do you need to say to each other? What can you learn from this situation? How can you respond differently if this happens again? When you've come up with a solution, let me know. I'm sure you guys can work this out!"

Sure enough, Nathan and Matt went off, talked together, and resolved the conflict. Nathan acknowledged that being teased was no fun, and Matt decided that, while it sure felt good to throw the boot, it would be better to just walk away or to come to one of us and ask for help.

Of course similar incidents did happen again, but over time we've made progress in helping our sons develop the awareness that there are always options for expressing our frustration and anger. These were opportunities to help them validate the reality of their own emotions, while at the same time to recognize that other people had valid emotions, too. Another seed planted, another truth reinforced, another healthy example modeled. And the next time this kind of conflict erupts, maybe, just maybe, it will be resolved a little more quickly and with a little less parental energy.[8]

Teaching about how to handle angry emotions is best done in a friendly way when you are less annoyed. Role-playing is a good idea if you can make a game out of it:

- "Remember show-and-tell? When you are really angry or sad or upset about something, please tell me how you feel, but don't show it by yelling or calling people names or by stomping your feet or throwing things."

- "Let's pretend you are very mad at me about something. Can you say, 'Dad, I'm real mad right now,' instead of yelling at me?"

- "A friend of mine didn't know what to say when his son was very angry about something. What advice should I give him?" By referring to a third party, you make the topic less personal. That might make it easier for your child to offer his opinion.[9]

Suggested Learning Activities for Preschoolers and Elementary-Age Children

1. Anger—what is it?

   Let's give it a color: _____

   Let's give it a sound: _____

   Let's give it a smell: _____

2. What does your body say when you get angry?

   What do you look like when you get angry?_____

   _____

   What does Mom look like when she gets angry?_____

   _____

   What does Dad look like when he gets angry?_____

   _____

3. Why do I get angry?

   Mom didn't let me see my friends.   Yes / No

   I struck out three times.   Yes / No

Some big guys were staring at me.   Yes / No

I hit my finger with the hammer.   Yes / No

I didn't get the video game I wanted.   Yes / No

Dad said I had to go to bed in the middle
of the TV show.   Yes / No

Other:_____   Yes / No

Answer: None of these makes us angry! We think other people make us angry, but they don't. We do! We make ourselves angry!

4. Here are three important words. Do they mean anything to you? What?

Frustration: _____

Fear: _____

Hurt: _____

5. What do you say when you are angry? (It doesn't have to be out loud!)

"She's stupid."   Yes / No

"She's crazy."   Yes / No

"She's bad."   Yes / No

"Jerk!"   Yes / No

"#@&!"   Yes / No

"Dummy."   Yes / No

But are people really like this? Would you say this about them if you were not angry at them?

When you get angry, what do *you* do? _____
(Pout, sit on the floor and kick my feet, throw my toys, nothing, get quiet and won't talk, glare, make signs at people behind their back.)

What will you do the next time you get angry?_____

_____

_____

6. "What have I heard about anger? Let me see…hmmm."

<u>Yes</u>   <u>No</u>

"Anger is bad."

"Never get angry."

"Anger makes you strong."

"Anger makes people go away from you."

"Anger eats a hole in your stomach."

"Good kids don't get angry."

7. Anger is a cover-up, a mask. It's like camouflage paint. Do you know what a disguise is? Sure you do. You try to hide who you are by wearing different clothing, or you paint your face with paint and wear camouflage clothes. Have you dressed up like this for school? For a party? For Halloween? I think we all have.

Did you know that people disguise their anger? It's true. Some kids or even adults do this from time to time.

Have you ever felt like being stubborn? You know what that is, don't you? Some kids show their anger by being stubborn. That is a disguised anger.

Have you ever forgotten to do something you were supposed to do? I have. Yup, it even happens to grown-ups, too. We have all forgotten. But you know what? Some people forget to show they are angry. They will not admit they are angry. They just "forget" and get back at the other person that way. That is a disguise, too.

There are many other disguises. Let's see if you can think of some:

1. _____

2. _____

3. _____

4. _____

What about joking? You can hide an angry, hurtful remark with a funny remark. And if your friend says, "That hurt," you say, "I was just kidding."

What about acting confused, like saying, "Gee, I didn't understand what you wanted," when we do understand? Our "mad" comes out this way.

Another one is, "Oh, I'm so tired" (yawn). You act tired so your brother or sister whom you are mad at has to do your work.

Another disguise is to pretend you are deaf. Some kids disguise their anger by saying, "I didn't hear you." You did hear what was said, but you think this is a good, safe way to show your anger.

Being clumsy is another way to show you are angry. You know, you *accidentally* break your sister's toy on purpose.

These are disguises. Why do kids show their anger these ways? Maybe it is safer. Other people do not like it when you say you are angry. Maybe it is the way you learned to be angry, but there are better ways to do it. Let's learn what they are.

8. What can I do to change my anger?
   — I will bury my anger. "I'm not angry." ("Ouch! My tummy hurts.")
   — I will throw my anger at other people. "Uh-oh, where did all my friends go?"
   — I will find the cause, solve the problem, get the anger out, and learn.

   Try to learn and memorize these Scriptures:
   "He who is slow to anger has great understanding, but he who is hasty of spirit exposes and exalts his folly" (Proverbs 14:29).
   "He who is slow to anger is better than the mighty, and he who rules his [own] spirit than he who takes a city" (Proverbs 16:32).
   "Good sense makes a man restrain his anger, and it is his glory to overlook a transgression or an offense" (Proverbs 19:11).
   "A [self-confident] fool utters all his anger, but a wise man keeps it back and stills it" (Proverbs 29:11).

9. It is not me that's angry—they are!
   "Uh-oh, I don't like their anger."
   "They started it."
   "Billy woke up on the wrong side of the bed, not me!"

10. What happens with anger?
    When people do not try to control their anger, they get into trouble—big trouble. Trouble with a capital T. They say

things and do things they wish they could take back. Has that ever happened to you? Have you ever said something and turned right around and said, "I take that back"? Sometimes you can't. That is why you need to stop and think when you are angry.

Good Ways to Handle Anger

Imagine you went to a friend's home. You are there for dinner. Your friend and his dad get into an argument. His dad gets madder and madder. He does not want his son to spend any more time with you. He does not ever want him to help you. He gets *so* mad he grabs a spear off the wall and throws it at his son. That will never happen, you say! Well, it did. It happened to David and his best friend Jonathan. "Then Saul became very angry with Jonathan… You son of a evil and disobedient woman! I know you are on the side of David….Then Saul threw his spear at Jonathan, trying to kill him" (1 Samuel 20:30,33 NCV).

Wow! That is anger out of control. You would not want to be around someone like that, would you? Saul did not think first. He did not think at all!

Someone else in the Bible got really angry, and he was *right* in getting angry. A lot of poor, homeless people were taken advantage of by important people. They took what little the poor had. It was not fair, so they complained to this man by the name of Nehemiah. Here is what he did:

> When I heard their complaints about these things, I was very angry. I thought about it. Then I accused the important people and leaders….The leaders were quiet. They

had nothing to say....They said, "We will give it back and not demand anything more from them. We will do as you say" (Nehemiah 5:6-12 NCV).

Wow! He was calm and cool. He was smart. He used his anger in a good way. You can do this, too. When you are angry, you could tell your friends and your folks, "I'm going to think before I say anything." And when you do, you will be putting the Bible into practice in your life.

"A person who controls his temper stops a quarrel" (Proverbs 15:18 NCV).

What are three steps you could take to control your anger?

1. _____

2. _____

3. _____

6

The Fear
of a Child

"I'm afraid. I don't want to go."

"I'm scared. He's too big."

"My stomach has butterflies in it."

"There's something under my bed!"

Where does fear come from? Do children learn to be afraid or is it innate? Our English word *fear* comes from the old English word *faer,* meaning "sudden calamity or danger." It has come to mean the emotional response to real or imagined danger. The Hebrew word for *fear* can also be translated as *dread,* meaning a heavy, oppressive sensation of fear. A word we often interchange with *fear* is *anxiety,* which comes from the Latin *anxias.* To be anxious is to be troubled in mind about some uncertain event. A variation of *anxias* means "to press tightly or to strangle." Anxiety is often a suffocating experience.

Fear and anxiety are actually quite similar. A real fear has an identifiable object of danger, either real (a burglar in the house) or imagined (a shadow that looks like a burglar). When we are anxious, we have the same feeling of fear, but we do not know why. The danger is subconscious. A child's imagination can create fears.

We live in a society in which it is easy to perceive danger. Any childhood experience that threatens a child's security and generates fear or threat can lead to an anxiety disorder. Here are some examples of these experiences:

- Seeing a gun or weapon
- Watching violence on television or in movies
- Divorce of parents
- Violence in the home (often associated with alcoholism)
- Theft of personal property
- Becoming sick and vomiting
- A serious or painful injury
- Ongoing parental sickness
- Sexual or physical abuse (this is a trauma which also arrests the emotional development of the child)
- Being bullied in school
- Natural disaster (hurricane, flood, fire, etc.)
- Terrorism or war[1]

According to some studies, up to 19 percent of children in the United States carry guns or other weapons to school, and up to 50 students each year are killed in school. To protect students, some schools employ guards and weapon-detection systems similar to the equipment used for airport security. Even if a child never witnesses an incident, being searched and inspected for weapons is enough to raise anxiety. In fact, 71 percent of eighth- and ninth-grade students worry about being shot or stabbed in school, according to a national survey.[2]

Were you aware that about 50 percent of children have six to seven signs of anxiety? These cover a multitude of concerns and include fear of animals, fear of thunder or lightning, and even fear of medical procedures such as injections.

Some children spend much of their time worrying. They pick up on every frightening event in the newspaper, in a book, or on television and relate it to themselves. Once they start worrying about something, they cannot seem to stop. Rather than putting the frightening event in perspective and letting it go, they often go to their parents with a series of "what if" questions:

> Child: What if burglars break into our house?
>
> Parent: It's not going to happen. The doors are locked.
>
> Child: But what if it does?
>
> Parent: We'll call the police.
>
> Child: But what if the burglars cut the telephone lines?
>
> Parent: The dog will scare them off.
>
> Child: But what if they kill the dog?
>
> Parent: It's not going to happen, Okay?
>
> Child: But what if...
>
> Parent: Stop this! You are being ridiculous![3]

Worried children think differently from the way the average child thinks. They seem to have a kind of radar for danger, perceiving it everywhere and remembering only the most frightening and upsetting aspects of many situations. Researchers have found that worriers of all ages show this selective memory for what is frightening. In addition, they tend to underestimate their own ability to cope with situations, resulting in even greater fear. Finally, most of the time they do not live in the present. Their focus is either on reviewing past (perceived) failures in themselves or on anticipating potential disasters in the future. Worries prevent them from enjoying or even paying attention to many events happening around them at the moment.[4]

How would you define *worry*? What sets it apart from anxiety or fear? When you experience anxiety, your body is responding. There is usually a muscle tightness and your heart is racing. *Worry* has been defined as "the *thinking* part of anxiety," as a series of thoughts and images that are full of emotion—but all negative. These thoughts are rarely uncontrollable, but they focus on something that has an uncertain outcome. The worrier is convinced beyond a shadow of a doubt that the outcome will be negative.

Worry comes from an Anglo-Saxon root meaning "to strangle" or "to choke." Worry is the uneasy, suffocating feelings we often experience in times of fear, trouble, or problems. When we worry, we look pessimistically into the future and think of the worst possible outcomes to the situations of our lives.

Worry is thinking turned into poisoned thoughts. It has been described as a small trickle of fear that meanders through the mind until it cuts a channel into which all other thoughts are drained.

Worry is a special kind of fear. To create it, we elongate fear with two things: anticipation and memory. We then infuse fear with our imagination and feed it with emotion. And then we have our creation.[5]

When you worry excessively, your brain is heavily impacted. The more you worry about something (and I mean hours a day, week after week), it is as though one of your brain's "switching stations" gets stuck. Have you ever had a cramp in your leg muscle, and it stayed and stayed regardless of what you did? Well, it is as though you have a brain cramp, and it will not let go of your worry. The more you worry, the more you cut a groove in your brain, and the more worry finds a home in which to reside. That is why other people's suggestions of "Don't worry" or "Just relax" will not work.

What do your children worry about? Do you know? Have you asked? If they are between the ages of 7 and 15, your children probably worry about school performance, appearance, social acceptance, death of a parent, and how their friends treat them. Some children also worry about world hunger and poverty, violence, and nuclear destruction.[6]

Our language is rich in terms that describe fear, anxiety, and related emotional responses. *Timidity* describes a continual tendency toward fear. *Panic* is the word for a sudden upsurge of terror. Consider the following terms in the vocabulary of fear. Which of these best describes your children's feelings when fear strikes? Place a check by each one.

apprehension	horror	anguish
worry	concern	edginess
wary	upset	agitation
trepidation	dread	alarm
uneasiness	disquiet	misgiving
jitteriness	unnerved	aghast
perturbation	scared	terror
panic	nervousness	solicitude
qualm	sensitivity	unsettled
distress	consternation	fright

What were your fears when you were a child? Do you remember?

Does fear have a purpose? It is a protective response. It helps us adapt and adjust to potential danger. It keeps us alive and well.

Children learn through experience what they need to fear. They need to anticipate the danger of certain situations, such as fire and other things that can burn, sharp objects, unsafe structures, or a pet that is being mistreated. Actually, the list is endless. Children respond in different ways to danger. Given the same circumstances, one child perceives a threat and another of the same age does not. It depends on several factors, but remember that *underreaction* in potential danger can be as harmful as *overreaction.*

Different Responses Relating to Gender

There seems to be a difference between boys and girls when it comes to who might be the most fearful. Most studies indicate that girls report having a greater number of fears, as well as more intense fears than boys! Some have explained this as innate, just a gender difference. But it is more likely that experiences and environment have a lot to do with the differences. Our society has determined that boys and girls should respond quite differently to fear. Early on, these patterns are learned from parents, teachers, siblings, friends, and television.[7]

Girls are given more freedom and encouragement to admit being afraid and to express their fears. Parents tend to be more cautious and restrictive with their daughters than their sons. And when daughters express their fears, they are likely to gain more support and comfort than a son would. Does this happen in your home?

Boys are encouraged to be more masculine and courageous. Fathers tend to be upset when their sons show fear, so they often act quickly to put a damper on its expression. Unfortunately, if a boy cannot express his fear directly, it may come out in stuttering, depression, asthma, or sleep disorders.

Fear at Different Stages of Development

Children's fears change as they grow older. That is because their experiences change, as evidenced by the isolated life of the newborn and the exploratory behavior of the active two-year-old. As children grow older, their thinking, reasoning, and vocabulary abilities expand—and so does their potential for fear. The more they explore, the more cautions and warnings they receive, and the more hurts they experience firsthand. We go from saying, "Be careful riding your tricycle," to "Be careful riding your bike in the street," to "Be careful with the car tonight. Watch out for…."

What about toddlers? Their fears are related to immediate situations. But preschoolers have a memory to draw from and may anticipate what could happen in the future. Life is scary for them, but much of this fear is in their imaginations. Two- to four-year-old children's most common fears are of the dark, being alone, and imaginary creatures. My friend Gary told me about the reaction his two boys had when they saw the movie *Jaws* at ages nine and six. It was too real to them. Recently, I saw the Disney film *Fantasia* for the first time since I was a child. All I remembered was enjoying it when I was young. I loved the animation and music, but I could see how scary some of the sequences might be for very young children.

Newborns and toddlers feel secure with the familiar. It is the new, the strange, and the unexpected that can trigger a fear response. Perhaps you have seen the fear of strangers in the face of your infant. Whenever our pastor conducts an infant dedication, I watch the expression on the child's face. At times when the parents are handing the child to him, a look of wide-eyed, stark terror comes over the infant's face. It is just a normal response for children of this age.

After about six months of age, most children begin to develop a fear commonly referred to as *separation distress*.[8] When children are alone but know Mom is somewhere around, they are comfortable. But when they cannot find her, they may raise the roof with their cries. When they have a prolonged separation like hospitalization or abandonment, the fear and anxiety they experience can follow them throughout their lives. We have worked with numerous adults who struggle with this fear of abandonment, and it usually developed in their childhood. Separation distress is one of those childhood fears that does not go away like so many others. It simply changes its form of expression.

As children move out of the infancy stage, two new fears can emerge: a school phobia and a death phobia. We use the term *phobia* when describing an intense fear. All kids have some level of fear, but when they try every way possible to avoid something (like going to school), the fear may have become phobic.[9]

There are many other fears children experience. Some of the most common fears are animals and insects (children are more afraid of dogs than cats), the dark, death, doctors, dentists (I remember this one!), heights, dreams and nightmares, fantasy creatures and monsters, school, storms, and deep water.[10]

Fears may take many forms and be expressed in several ways. As children move through the school years, their fears are often individualized, depending on their own life experience. Acts of violence portrayed on television or real-life tragedies or losses feed their fears. Some common fears which many kids experience relate to their social relationships and individual competence.[11] Children notice their differences and compare themselves to other children. They are vulnerable to the typical responses of ridicule and rejection, and no matter what their age, it hurts. What about you? Did you ever experience the agony of being the last person chosen for a team? When the seeds of inferiority are planted, they tend to grow until the child's life is lived with a constant fear.[12]

Fears and Temperaments

Why are some children more afraid than others? Are all fears learned, or is there an inborn tendency to be fearful? Every child enters the world with certain predispositions. These personality characteristics are often referred to as temperaments. Even from birth, there are some babies who are referred to as easy and some as difficult. We really do not fully understand why some children are like this, except there is some evidence that genetics plays a role, as well as the emotional state of the mother during pregnancy. Yes, it is true. Babies do tend to be affected by the emotional and physical stress of the mother.[13] These are not just offhand opinions or labels but a determination based on the baby's responses to bathing, cuddling, feeding, and dressing.

But what is the difference? Difficult babies' patterns of eating, sleeping, and elimination are not regular or predictable from day to day as the easy babies' are. They do not adapt easily to new people or situations. Change upsets them, and fussing is usually the result. Crying is frequent and often without any identifiable cause. And it is not a quiet cry. It is usually wailing and screaming. Parents can become weary and frustrated since nothing they try works. These children tend to have a wider and more intense range of emotional responses. Because of this, a difficult child is more vulnerable to being fearful. Fortunately, only a small number of children fit this profile.

What about your child? What are his or her fears? Do you know? Have you asked? Take a moment to reflect on this.

7

Where Do Their Fears Come From?

Children are not born with fear. They learn to be afraid. It is developed; therefore, much of it is preventable. How do children develop fear? Experience is one way. One single traumatic event may be all it takes for that fear to gain a foothold and hang on for dear life. And if this upsetting experience is repeated again and again, it can become much stronger. For instance, if a child eats a piece of fruit and becomes ill, she may have a fear of eating that fruit again. Another child may have had an accident while visiting the zoo. Now every time his parents suggest visiting the zoo, fear begins to build.

Years ago one of the girls in my high school group shared with me her experience with cats. As a young child, she was riding her tricycle around the block. Suddenly, a cat emerged from inside one of the houses, attacked her, and scratched her leg. After that, every time she saw a cat, or someone suggested getting her one, she became terrified. When I met her, the fear was so intense that if someone brought a cat into the room, she would literally bolt out the door.

I had my tonsils taken out when I was six years old. My doctor told me I would be in the hospital for two or three days, and I could eat a lot of sherbet. But my adenoids bled for a week, and I had a very unpleasant experience. For years, whenever I would visit the doctor's office and smell the same hospital smells, I experienced a sense of anxiety.

When these fears are not dealt with, children will generalize them to other situations or objects, and they can be carried into adult life. We have had parents ask us why their child is afraid of a specific item or situation. They are confused because the child has never been exposed to it or had a bad experience with it. Children's fears are often generalized to other things or experiences. A child who was attacked by a rooster while visiting a farm soon reacts with fear to most feathered animals, even stuffed animals. A child who accidentally locked herself in her closet soon refuses to go into any small room, and wants to leave the door open to both the bathroom and her bedroom. Another child, startled by a train whistle near his grandmother's home, fell off his bike. Since then, he jumps at any loud, piercing sound and often begins to cry. The next year, he threw a tantrum when his parents tried to take him on a train in an amusement park.

Children Who Acquire Fear from Their Parents

How do children learn to be afraid? They may actually learn some of their fears from us. Children learn through modeling and imitative learning. They like to imitate adults who are important to them. I may tell my child not to be afraid of going to the doctor, but if he sees me sitting anxiously in the waiting room, palms sweating, thinking of ways to cancel the appointment, he will know I am afraid.

When children are preschool age, they develop a fine-tuned antenna that picks up fear in other people. This is an important skill because it helps them protect themselves when real danger exists. But the downside is that it gives children another way to develop unnecessary fears. Children respect and admire their parents. They see them as competent and strong problem-solvers who protect them from danger. When children see fear in their parents, they tend to adopt those fears and phobias as their own.[1]

One of the places children observe fear or fright is on television. TV is an extremely strong source of observational learning. It presents many unrealistic and exaggerated situations that tend to frighten children. It can actually initiate a fear of dangerous situations that are unlikely to ever happen to the child. If children watch a lot of the mayhem portrayed on TV, they begin to believe that what they see is realistic, and that it could happen to them. Because of its emphasis on negative reporting, even newscasts fall into this category. Many of today's films and reality shows can create fears and phobias as well. These problems can often be overcome by parents watching and discussing the program with their kids. Unfortunately, parents often have no idea what their kids are watching.

The Power of Imagination

One of the greatest gifts we are born with is our imagination. We use it to create fantasies and daydreams. All of the world's best (and worst) ideas and inventions had their beginnings in someone's imagination. We can use our imagination in a positive or negative way. This ability to form mental pictures, including fearful ones, has tremendous power. But a fearful image can sometimes interfere with reality. All of us are born with a sin nature, and unfortunately, it can affect a child's imagination at an early age.

Many children between the ages of two and five years old have imaginary companions with whom they play and talk. They cannot yet distinguish between what is real and what is imaginary. It is normal and appropriate behavior for them to even call on their imaginary friends to help them when they are afraid. But the same imagination children use to deal with fears can also create them.

John was a boy with numerous fears. His mother could not come up with any reasons to explain why he had become like this. After several sessions of counseling, his therapist was able to discover that his fears came from some imagined events that John, with his limited abilities, thought were real.[2] Young children often engage in imaginings like this, which we call magical thinking.

Children Who Lack the Confidence to Handle Danger

Another source of fear in small children is that they feel helpless in the face of actual danger. As children grow, they need to discover that they do have the ability to take care of themselves. Children who lack this belief, or fail to receive encouragement to develop this confidence, are prone to having fears. These children can become afraid before anything actually happens.[3] They eventually see themselves as weak and less capable or experienced. Fear begins to take over and eventually dominates their lives. Whenever children experience ongoing feelings of shame, anxiety, and inferiority, they may construct a vicious cycle that aggravates the problem. The fear becomes a self-fulfilling prophecy.

Ted is a nine-year-old who is extremely gifted at playing the piano, but he lives with the fear of making a mistake while performing. At a recital last year, his fingers fumbled on the keys, causing him to lose his place. He was unable to finish the piece. To make matters worse, the same thing has happened twice since then. Now he lives with the constant dread of this happening again.

His fear has grown so big in his mind that it actually affects his ability to perform.

Parents often ask me why their children's fears continue. We all tend to perpetuate our fears by inadvertently feeding them. For example, every time we avoid or run from something we fear, we give it power and control over us. If we, as adults, with our well-developed resources do this, imagine how easily our kids fall into this trap.

Many things influence a child's fears. Temperament, experiences, thoughts, and imagination all play a part. For illustration's sake, consider a hypothetical case created by Dr. Edward Sarafino. The boy's name is Alan, and he is afraid of birds. Imagine with me what this child's life would be like if all of the following conditions existed:

- He was born with a difficult temperament, making him less able to handle stressful events.

- His parents are impatient, frustrated, or infuriated when he reacts fearfully to birds.

- He later walks under a tree and birds swoop toward him trying to protect their nest.

- He has a painful experience or suffers an injury that relates to birds.

- He avoids birds (for instance, by staying indoors a lot).

- His fearfulness leads to secondary gains, such as not having to help with outdoor chores.

- His friends are afraid of birds, too.

- He sees birds attack people on TV or in the movies.

- He sees a horror movie that exaggerates the size and power of birds (for instance, an enormous bird that devours a city).

- He sees a realistic film showing the predatory activities of eagles and pelicans and then thinks he could become the victim.

- He is warned to stay away from a caged bird because it will bite him.

- He has nightmares about birds and thinks these dreams are real events.

- He has no imaginary companion to rely on for emotional protection and support.

- He develops a negative self-concept and feels a sense of helplessness in stressful situations.[4]

Do you see why Alan might be full of fear? Using fears your own children might be dealing with, ask yourself which conditions might exist for them that may feed their fears. Keep in mind that whenever more than one of these conditions exists, your children's fears will compound and become exaggerated.

Parents Reward Children for Showing Fear

Unfortunately, another way kids learn to fear is by being rewarded for their fear. Perhaps a parent allows children to get out of certain responsibilities or obligations because of fear. Or maybe they learn that they can get a lot of attention from parents and friends by appearing fearful. Some children exaggerate their fear because of the attention they receive. I have seen children walk into a yard with a small dog and be perfectly at ease when no adults are present. The same children with the same dog may behave much differently when adults are there to see their fear. They have been known to stop or start crying, depending on whether or not a parent is watching. Parents can condition their children's fears by paying too much attention to their behavior.

Recognizing Your Children's Fears

How do you recognize your children's fears? What are the indications that anxiety is present? Some children are very verbal about their fears, and you have little difficulty becoming aware of them. Other children either avoid thinking about them or make it a point not to share their fears. But if children are quite fearful or troubled by anxiety, you might begin to notice some of the following symptoms emerging:

- difficulty concentrating
- listlessness or hyperactivity
- appetite changes—either eating very little or too much
- bedwetting
- nightmares
- restlessness
- insomnia
- overly talkative or not talking at all
- stuttering
- panic attacks
- compulsive behavior
- obsessive patterns
- physical complaints

Dealing with Fear of Animals

Let's look in more detail at some of these childhood fears and what can be done about them. For many children, an animal is an object of fear (for many adults as well). How do you help children who are afraid of an animal? First, realize that they lack the ability to cope with their fear all at once. Do not try to force them to face it suddenly.

Let's say the fear is of cats. Although cats look harmless, their claws are sharp. A cat may appear small to us, but think of it from a child's perspective. A 30-pound child sees a 15-pound cat differently than a grown-up does. Imagine a cat that is half of your weight, and your response might be a bit more cautious. A cat can also bite and be unpredictable.

Try the following approach when dealing with the fear of animals with your child. Begin by gradually giving your child exposure to the animal. First, show your child pictures of a cat or point out certain qualities of cats on television or in a book. Let your child observe you enjoy handling a cat or looking at the picture of a cat. Let the child know he can pet the cat as you do. Do not force him, but when he does touch the cat, talk about how soft the cat's fur is, how pretty it is, etc. It is important to select a cat that is calm and responds positively to love and attention. Encourage your child to pet the cat with you more and more frequently. The time will come when he is able to do this on his own and be spontaneous about it.

Some parents have found it is helpful to have their children keep a written record of their progress regarding whatever it is they fear. Such a written record shows children they are attaining a goal. The record might indicate when they responded to a cat, how long, where, and their positive feelings.

Dealing with Fears of the Night

Our minds run wild during sleep. Darkness can be frightening—it can generate fears of being isolated, left alone, abandoned, or being lost.

Nightmares and fears of ghosts and such are common childhood concerns. They are different from fears of animals or bugs or heights that are purely in the mind of the child; whereas, a child with a fear of dogs may actually have been bitten. It is easy to prove to a child that a daddy longlegs is harmless (though perhaps quite yucky). It is harder to convince a child that ghosts are not real or that bad dreams will not return.

Things to Consider

Fears of the dark or of monsters under the bed are typical of preschoolers. If your child outgrew those fears but is suddenly complaining about them, look into this. The reason may be simple (Did she watch a scary movie?), or there may be deeper concerns (Did a relative die recently and your child is worried about ghosts?).

Repetitive nightmares (those that continue over a few weeks) are a sign of some distress. Look for the obvious stresses such as a new school, a serious illness of a member of the family, marital fighting, etc.

If a child is over age seven and struggles with separation anxiety, he may experience nightmares more than kids without separation anxiety. Your child may want to sleep elsewhere. This may be okay for one night. Many children are fine by the next day. Beyond that, you need to try alternative means to help your child get over her fears.

Here is what you can say to your child:

> "Most children feel this way once in a while. And they discover that if they try to think of more fun thoughts, they eventually go back to sleep."

> "Nightmares can be very scary. Even though they're not real, they feel real. Some people have said, 'I discovered that wasn't real.' Everybody gets nightmares,

and everybody eventually learns to go to sleep after having one."

"You've been feeling scared a lot lately. I wonder what might be bothering you?"

Sometimes you need to negotiate with your child:

"You're worried about going to bed tonight. Last night you slept with us. Tonight you can go back to your bed. If you want, I'll stay outside your door for a few minutes. What do you want me to do?"

"You just had a nightmare. It is scary but won't hurt you. I'll sit with you for a while, and you'll begin to notice that you are feeling better."

"You just had a nightmare. What have you done before when you've been bothered by this?"

Another way to handle bad dreams is to consciously decide to dream differently. At bedtime, help the child come up with things that he wants to dream about other than the subject of his nightmares.

Another tack to take with recurrent bad dreams is to imagine a different ending. If a child has survived a car crash and keeps dreaming about the moment of impact, have her imagine Superman swooping down at the scene of the accident and carrying the car off to safety. Though dreams are not the stuff of the conscious mind, you'll be surprised how much control your child can have over them.[5]

How Not to Say It

Here are common mistakes we all make in what we say when we feel frustrated that our child is not overcoming nighttime fear.

"It's the middle of the night. How many times do I have to tell you there are no such things as ghosts?"

"You have to be brave."

"Oh, now what? I told you not to watch that program!"

If a child comes from a divorced household, it is difficult, but critical, that both parents work together with the same approach to alleviate the child's fears. One household may allow the light to be on, a pet in the room, or sleeping with the parent, while the other household may not. One home may be patient and understanding about the fear, and the other household is angry and impatient with the child. Which home would the child prefer to sleep at? Often, this is not considered.

Once again, a gradual approach can be helpful with a child. Children need to know that it is all right to talk about their fears, that we will not make fun of them for being fearful. You might try gradually reducing the amount of light in their rooms at night. Share with them Proverbs 3:24-26, and help them commit it to memory:

> When you lie down, you shall not be afraid; yes, you shall lie down, and your sleep shall be sweet. Be not afraid of sudden terror and panic, nor of the stormy blast or the storm and ruin of the wicked when it comes [for you will be guiltless], for the Lord shall be your confidence, firm and strong and shall keep your foot from being caught [in a trap or some hidden danger].

If your children struggle with nighttime fears, here are some ways you can help them overcome their fears.

1. *Let your children know that it is all right to be afraid.* Everyone has fears at some time in their life. A certain amount of fear is normal, and we do not have to be ashamed when we are afraid. By doing this, you can reduce your children's feelings of guilt and

shame. Share your own childhood fears, and let your children know that those fears passed in your life. This can be an encouragement to them.

2. *Help your children understand that being afraid is temporary.* They may even fear that they will be afraid forever. Give them a message of hope for the future, that will in turn create an expectation of success.

3. *Let your children know that it is perfectly all right to talk about their fear.* Sharing their fear helps them keep it in perspective. It helps if you know the extent of their fear in order to help them overcome any distortions they may have. Many parents have found it helpful if their children draw their feelings on paper or act out their fantasies, or use puppets to talk out their fears.

Sometimes children are fearful, but they have difficulty articulating what it is they are afraid of. It may be because they are too upset or do not have the verbal skills to adequately express themselves. It is not productive to try forcing fear out of them or shaming them into telling you. Your best bet is patience and observation. You may find it helpful to keep a log of the times your children are afraid. By comparisons, you can discover a pattern that will help you identify the source of their fear. Counselors often use picture books, allowing kids to point to whatever they are afraid of. Or they can use dolls to act out the situation. You might also try the sentence-completion approach where you make up a sentence but leave the ending unfinished, so the child finishes it for you.[6]

4. *Let your children know that it is also normal not to be afraid.* When kids can observe another person not being afraid in a situation that scares them, they get the message that it is possible not to be afraid.

5. *Help your children learn a new response or behavior to replace their fear response.* These are called counter behaviors or fear-replacing behaviors. Encourage your children to imagine themselves not being afraid in a situation that would normally frighten them. Positive imageries are powerful substitutes. Participating in a positive activity or favorite pastime during a fearful situation can eventually lessen the fear.

As with adults, so it is with kids: Repeatedly facing our fears is the best method of overcoming them. When children avoid a feared object, this actually strengthens the fear. Children get relief by avoiding or escaping a scary situation and believe that such relief can only occur in that way. So they will continue the avoidance behavior.

Your children can overcome a strong fear by learning that certain situations are not as threatening as they once believed (for example, dogs can be friendly). Children can discover they can cope with this uncertainty by staying in the situation long enough for the doubts and fears to begin to go away. It may take your encouragement for this to happen. (Make sure you teach your children appropriate caution. No one should ever approach a strange dog with sudden movements or loud noises or by running up to it.)

What can you say to your child when he is afraid? Why not ask your child, "What's your worst fear?" and offer comfort and reassurance. "You're afraid the dog will bite you or knock you down. He is very friendly, but he can get excited and jump sometimes. Just because you feel scared doesn't mean there is really something to be afraid about."

You could teach coping with a fear by modeling new responses: "I'm going to pet the dog and let it lick my hand. Watch."

You could try the gradual approach: "You can watch the dog and me from the window. That way you'll feel safe. After a while you can watch me from the porch. Then you can watch me close-up."

And you can help your child understand that his fear is temporary: "You did that very well. It isn't easy to do something that makes you nervous, but you did. I'm sure you'll be able to do that again."

We need to teach our children to tap the creative powers of their God-given imaginations to see themselves in their own mind handling their greatest fears.

8
Preparing Your Children to Avoid the Fears of Life

If parents can anticipate some of the most obviously fearful situations in their children's lives and address them in advance, it gives their children reassurance. For instance, many children are afraid of the first day of school, going away to camp, going to stay with a relative, going to the doctor or hospital, and so on. By telling your children where they are going, letting them know what to expect, and discussing how to handle the situation, they will feel much more comfortable and less likely to use their imaginations in a negative, fearful manner.

As a child, I went into the hospital when I was six, and again at nine. I do not remember much about either experience except that one of these visits was an emergency. Some children have to be rushed in, while others have plenty of time to think about the experience. You may think your child has no concern over the upcoming event because the child appears nonchalant and tells you that it is no big deal. Let your child know that some concern or apprehension is normal, then share some of your own experiences, allowing them an opportunity to talk about their fears.

Steps to Fear-Proofing Your Children

Raymond was seven years old and had developed gum problems. His dentist recommended pulling several of his teeth. Raymond had only been to his dentist a few times for checkups and cleaning. His parents did not want him to develop fear associated with going to the dentist office, so here is what they did to prepare him for the extractions.

1. Both his mother and father sat down and shared with him that this visit was going to be different. (Fortunately, his parents were not the kind who complained about their visits and how much pain they had experienced at the hands of their dentist.) They told him they would both be there and described what the dentist would be doing. They told him he could ask any questions of them or of the dentist.

2. They shared some of their own experiences and portrayed a calm attitude for him.

3. They went to the dentist for an additional examination and X-rays. The nurse and dentist described the procedure and showed him some of the instruments. The dentist had Raymond pinch his own arm so he would understand what the Novocain would feel like. They described what his recovery would feel like and kept encouraging him to ask questions.

4. His parents talked with him about comments his friends would make about the procedure, and helped him think through what he would say to them if the comments were negative.

Parents who take their child to the hospital for an operation should follow a similar procedure. Public libraries and bookstores are gold mines of helpful materials, many written specifically for children.

Things to Avoid

How can parents help their children overcome fear? There are several steps you can take that will be helpful, but also a number of things to avoid.

1. *The forced approach is not helpful.* Some parents believe that forcing their children to face their fears is the best approach to take. Unfortunately, it tends to make the problem worse because your children's emotional response to the fear blocks the rationalization of logic or fact. A gradual desensitization process will work much better.

2. *Shaming or ridiculing only further aggravates your children's fears.* Many parents who feel frustrated or perhaps embarrassed by their children's demonstration of fear in front of other people, may respond by shaming or ridiculing their children. These parents may compare their children to others, communicating messages like, "Why can't you be a big boy like Fred? There's nothing to be afraid of. Rabbits are nice animals." We have to see fear through our children's eyes, even though we do not personally relate to the fear.

We have seen some parents actually punish their children for being afraid. The parents used demeaning terms against their children such as *bad, immature,* and *baby.* They threatened their children with isolation in their room or being sent away until they learn to act grown up and brave. This only compounds their fears because they now have to deal with the fear of abandonment as well. If this fear gains a foothold, it will follow them into adult life and pollute their relationships. Even schoolteachers can be guilty of reinforcing this problem by misinterpreting children's fears as misbehavior.

3. *Overprotecting your children keeps them from growing emotionally and learning to deal with fears.* While shopping, I recently observed an exchange between a mother and child that made me cringe. It was characteristic of the way many parents tend to overprotect their children. This mother was giving her daughter instructions, directions, and advice—most of which were not necessary. She reminded me of a hovercraft, and the child was obviously smothered by her. Children raised in this kind of environment tend to be helpless: *OK, if they want to shelter me and take care of me, I'll let everyone else do things for me throughout my life.*

The flip side of this are parents who ignore their children's fears and concerns. One father told me, "He'll just grow out of it. If I give him any attention, it will just make things worse. He'll learn." But how can children learn with their limited capabilities unless they receive guidance from someone who is more knowledgeable?

Things to Do

Now that we have covered some of the most obvious mistakes to avoid, let's look at specific things parents can do to help their children overcome their fears.

1. *Desensitization*—One of the best ways to help your children overcome their fears is through the process of desensitization. Understandably, many kids develop a fear of animals. I have a large golden retriever. He is a happy, loving, and friendly dog. He loves children, but I have had to teach him to lie down and wait for children to approach him. He has frightened several small children. Just imagine being three feet tall and watching a huge dog run toward you with his tail wagging frantically, and his tongue hanging out of a huge mouth with giant teeth. You would probably run and hide behind your mom, too. An experience like this

could trigger a crippling fear that would be generalized to other dogs and animals. This is where desensitization comes into play. It is a gradual process of facing fear through small, positive steps. The best way to begin overcoming a fear is to face it a little at a time, from a safe distance.

What are the steps involved in the process of desensitization? These must be small enough for your child to succeed, but they also need to be challenging. The following steps have worked for many people:

a) Give your child some voice as to when it is time to move on to the next step. Why? It increases your child's sense of control, which tends to reduce his fear. And then be sure you praise and encourage every success as well as effort. Do not push your child, and be sure you and your spouse are in agreement over this. A child's success can be hindered if parents do not work as a team.

b) The sooner your child confronts what he or she is afraid of, the faster these procedures work. You do not want anticipating anxiety to gain a foothold in your child's life.

c) The process of desensitization works, but only if the positives to what he is afraid of are not far apart. The best procedure is daily; otherwise, a child may look forward to those days when he can avoid his fears.

d) How long should a child stay in a feared situation? Research indicates it takes about 20 minutes for the anxiety to subside when a fear is confronted. Work toward this goal. Letting a child experience the situation and then leaving it right away is not a learning experience.

Expose your child to the same source of fear each time. Do not vary it in the slightest or it can lose its effect.[1]

2. *Scripture memorization*—Memorizing God's Word at an early age is a positive step toward eliminating fears. The phrase "fear not" is used 366 times in the Bible. Help your child memorize all or part of the following passages:

> Fear not…for I am with you; do not look around you in terror and be dismayed, for I am your God. I will strengthen and harden you to difficulties, yes, I will help you; yes, I will hold you up and retain you with My [victorious] right hand of rightness and justice (Isaiah 41:10).

> You will guard him and keep him in perfect and constant peace whose mind…is stayed on You, because he commits himself to You, leans on You and hopes confidently in You (Isaiah 26:3).

> But now…thus says the Lord, He Who created you, O Jacob, and He Who formed you, O Israel: Fear not, for I have redeemed you [ransomed you by paying a price instead of leaving you captives]; I have called you by your name; you are Mine. When you pass through the waters, I will be with you, and through the rivers, they will not overwhelm you. When you walk through the fire, you will not be burned or scorched, nor will the flame kindle upon you. For I am the Lord your God, the Holy One of Israel, your Savior; I give Egypt… for your ransom, Ethiopia and Seba…in exchange [for your release] (Isaiah 43:1-3).

> Casting the whole of your care [all your anxieties, all your worries, all your concerns, once and for all] on Him, for He cares for you affectionately, and cares about you watchfully (1 Peter 5:7).

3. *The use of imagination*—The use of imagination means helping your children see themselves safe in situations that might normally frighten them. For instance, in the case of a small boy

who has a fear of dogs, you might begin by looking at picture books that are about dogs or that feature a dog as the character in a story. You will need to review these books in advance, making sure they do not contain elements that might provoke or reinforce your child's fear.

Stuffed toys can be like encountering a small, docile dog. At first, it may be enough just to have the dog in the same room, or your child playing near a dog that cannot come in contact with him.

One mother kept a record of progress with her child. It looked something like this:

- **Monday:** Ken played in a room for a while with the dog in another room.
- **Tuesday:** The dog came into the same room and sat tied up for 5 minutes while Ken played.
- **Wednesday:** I petted the dog and played with it while Ken played with his toys. I mentioned that his mouth was opened and his tongue was out because he was smiling and happy.
- **Thursday:** I played with the dog, and Ken played on the other side of me.
- **Friday:** Ken petted the dog and the dog wagged his tail each time. I showed Ken how happy the dog was when he petted him.
- **Saturday:** Ken petted the dog and played with him for a few minutes.
- **Sunday:** Ken hugged the dog and played with him. He didn't seem to mind that the dog wiggled. He even touched some of his teeth and let the dog lick his fingers.

Keeping a log like this can help you plot the progress of your child.

4. *Make a plan*—In reducing any fear, it is important for you to think up several approaches. Actually, coming up with 15 or more steps is helpful, even if you do not use them all. Try to determine which steps are the most and the least fearful. Each step you take to expose your children to their fears should be a bit more fear-arousing than the previous one. Keep the steps gradual in their progression, and as kids master each step, let them know how far they have come. They need to build on their successes.

Do not expect immediate improvement. It will take several sessions of exposure (anywhere from a few moments to as much as 30 minutes each), to reduce a moderate fear. Be sure your children proceed at their own pace. Do not rush them. Try to end every encounter on a positive note. Begin each new encounter where they left off the day before. And above all, be flexible and willing to adapt and experiment.

Fear of the dark is a typical fear for many children. The following steps are effective in eliminating this fear:

1. Your child is in a room sitting with a friend and the lighting is fairly dim.

2. You and your child light two candles and you turn off all the electric lights.

3. You and your child are in the room together, and your child blows out one of the candles.

4. You and your child and a friend are in the room together. The friend blows out one candle, and your child blows out the remaining candle. You talk to each other while the room is dark. After 5 seconds, your child turns on an electric light.

5. You and your child repeat step 4, but this time you wait a full minute before turning on the light.

6. You and your child repeat step 4, but this time you wait 5 minutes before turning on the light.

7. Your child is alone in the room and the electric lighting is dim.

8. Your child is alone in the room and there are only two candles lit.

9. Your child is alone in the room and there is only one candle lit.

10. Your child is alone in the room and there is only one candle lit. Your child calls a friend on the phone, blows out the candle, and talks for a couple of minutes. Then she turns on the electric light and finishes her phone conversation.

11. Your child is alone in the room and there is one candle lit. She blows it out and waits 5 seconds before she turns on the electric light.

12. Your child repeats step 11, but this time she waits 20 seconds.

13. Your child repeats step 11, but this time she waits a full minute.

14. Your child repeats step 11, but this time she waits 5 full minutes.*

The number of steps may vary, depending on your child's needs. The more gradual the approach to the fear, the more steps you will want to include. Whatever fears your child may have, you can take the steps outlined here and structure a fear-reduction plan designed for each specific fear.

Helping Your Child with Worry

You can teach your children to give their thoughts and worries to God. Look at these principles and scriptures:

---

* This exercise is intended for children seven years old and up who are responsible enough to be around lit candles.

Center your thoughts on God, not on worry: "You will guard him and keep him in perfect and constant peace whose mind [both its inclination and its character] is stayed on You" (Isaiah 26:3). Whatever you choose to think about will either produce or dismiss feelings of anxiety and worry. Those people who suffer from worry are choosing to center their minds on negative thoughts and to anticipate the worst. But if your mind or imagination is centered on God—what He has done and will do for you—and the promises of Scripture, peace of mind is inevitable. But you must choose to center your thoughts in this way. God has made the provision, but *you must take the action.* Freedom from worry and anxiety is available, but you must lay hold of it.

Replace fretting with trust. Psalm 37 (NASB) begins, "Do not fret," and those words are repeated later in the psalm. The dictionary defines *fret* as "to eat away, gnaw, gall, vex, worry, agitate, wear away." The entire psalm is filled with reminders of the security of those who trust in the Lord instead of fretting.

Whenever I hear the word *fret,* I am reminded of the scene I see each year when I hike along the Snake River in the Grand Teton National Park in Wyoming. Colonies of beavers live along the riverbanks, and often I see trees at various stages of being gnawed to the ground by the beavers. Some trees have slight rings around their trunks where the beavers have just started to chew on them. Other trees have several inches of bark eaten away, and some have already fallen to the ground because the beavers have gnawed through the trunks. Worry has the same effect on us: It will gradually eat away at us until it destroys us.

In addition to telling us not to fret, Psalm 37 gives us positive substitutes for worry. First, it says, "Trust (lean on, rely on, and be confident) in the Lord" (verse 3). Trust is a matter of not attempting to live an independent life or to cope with difficulties alone. It means going to a greater Source for strength.

Second, verse 4 says, "Delight yourself also in the Lord." To delight means to rejoice in God and what He has done for us, to let God supply the joy for our life.

Third, verse 5 says, "Commit your way to the Lord." Commitment is a definite act of the will, and it involves releasing our worries and anxieties to the Lord.

And fourth, we are to "rest in the Lord; wait for Him" (verse 7). This means to submit in silence to what He ordains, and to be ready and expectant for what He is going to do in our life.

Stop worrying and start praying. The passage in Philippians 4:6-9 can be divided into three basic stages. We are given a *premise:* Stop worrying. We are given a *practice:* Start praying. And we are given a *promise:* God's peace will be ours. The promise is there and available, but we must follow the first two steps in order for the third to occur. We must stop worrying and start praying if we are to begin receiving God's peace. Psalm 34:1-4 is another Scripture passage on how praise and prayer lead to deliverance from the worries of life.

We do not live in a safe world anymore. We can worry about this, or we can live one day at a time. Jesus said,

> Therefore I will tell you, do not worry about your life, what you will eat or drink; or about your body, what you will wear. Is not life more important than food, and the body more important than clothes? Look at the birds of the air; they do not sow or reap or store away in barns, and yet your heavenly Father feeds them. Are you not much more valuable than they? Who of you by worrying can add a single hour to his life? (Matthew 6:25-27 NIV).

It helps in handling a child's worry (or yours) to identify what you can control in life and what you cannot. Even when upsets and bad things happen, the best approach is to focus on what can be done or controlled, and then commit the rest to the Lord. "Don't worry about anything; instead, pray about everything; tell God your needs and don't forget to thank him for his answers" (Philippians 4:6 TLB). Each child you have could differ in his or her worry pattern. Here are some suggestions on what to say to your child:

> "On days you aren't so worried, what do you say to yourself that keeps you from being scared?" [Identify the coping skills your child already has and build on these.]

> "Do you know how our dog sometimes barks at sounds because he thinks they are threatening? Well, the part of your body that causes you to worry is like that. It is barking to protect you from things that really are not problems. It is possible to train your mind not to be so overprotective."

> "You were worried about my safety today, but then you told yourself I would be fine and you prayed for me. I wonder what other things we could pray about."

Here are suggestions on what to avoid saying to your child:

> "You did it yesterday. Why don't you do it today?" ["Why" questions are not good. He may turn around and give you seven reasons "why." Remember, most intense fears are not overcome by one successful experience. Your child needs many successful experiences over a period of time. You could remind him of past successes, but do not push. Try for a smaller achievable goal. It is easier to play with a puppy or a newborn dog than it is to play with a grown dog.]

> "You're being a baby." [Avoid shaming. This won't help. And if your child does succeed, he will appreciate your help.]

"It's all right to avoid dogs if you don't like them."
[Avoidance will not teach him to overcome the fear.]

When Trauma Hits Your Child

I received a phone call one morning. My friend Mike said, "Norm, I hope you don't mind, but I gave your name to the principal of the middle school my daughter attends. You probably heard about that family in Irvine where the stepfather killed his wife and stepson. Well, his stepson was my daughter's friend and sat next to her. Her whole class is traumatized and needs help." These situations are happening more and more. It could not only happen in your area schools, but also in your church. The shootings at Columbine High School and Wedgewood Baptist Church in Texas are not isolated events.

When the twin towers in New York were destroyed, the tragedy was witnessed by students in Lower Manhattan's Stuyvesant High School. The school was evacuated and used for a while as a Ground Zero personnel center. Hundreds of these students gathered in Greenwich Village the Sunday after 9/11 and painted two giant commemorative murals to be mounted on their campus. They also created a commemorative issue of the student newspaper, *The Spectator*. The contributions to this paper actually were collective narratives of the kind found to be a healing element when a tragedy occurs. The following are some examples:

> A reporting of the traumatic event and the witnesses' part in it: "So what did you learn in school today?" On September 11, I gave a horribly truthful answer to this familiar question: "I learned that it is easy to tell a falling body from a falling piece of debris because bodies fall much faster." We stood in the ninth-floor chemistry lab for almost an hour, shocked by the sight of men and women in expensive clothes glancing back

into what was once their office before throwing themselves toward the chaotic sidewalk hundreds of feet below. Some appeared to have had a running start while others stood at the edge until the flames licked their skin and pushed them off into the endless cloud of smoke. Some held hands, while others preferred to dive alone into whatever fate followed that smoke.... Teachers' authority disappeared as each burst into hysterical tears. By ten o'clock, there were six teachers lined up next to the four of us, crying on each others' shoulders just like we were.[2]

Thoughts/feelings about the traumatic event and worldview: "It was shocking. It made you realize how vulnerable we are as a country, how unprepared. It was so easy to do what they did. The scariest part of it, for me, is that we're fighting an unconventional war.... There's no military base to bomb, no country to target.... I'm very doubtful of our ability to eliminate terrorism.[3]

In another traumatic event, in El Cajon, California, a high-school student opened fire with a shotgun on students and faculty, wounding four:

The principal used the public address system to announce the emergency and evacuate students. When school reopened, the faculty and staff noticed that students were responding with high anxiety whenever the principal would use the P.A. system. The principal began to make a daily practice of getting on the P.A. and wishing the students a good day. She would reassure them that all was well, and then she would proceed to the day's announcements. She noticed that this practice served to desensitize students to the sound of her voice on the P.A. and helped reduce their trauma-related anxiety.[4]

What are the results of trauma impacting adolescents? They are likely to engage in the following:

- They act out their distress through isolation, drug and alcohol abuse, sexual activity, violence, delinquency, running away, and suicidal expressions.
- They experience low self-esteem and are quick to blame themselves for the way they responded to the trauma.
- They seem to grow old too fast. Some develop lifestyles years ahead of where they should be.
- Their anger is often displaced toward people at school because they are safer than others.
- Their concern is with themselves. They will interpret an event on the basis of how it affects them.[5]

When adolescents experience a crisis or trauma, they often regress.

Traumatic events of any kind turn the life of a child upside down. To a child, trauma is like an ongoing, festering splinter, and fear can be an expected result.

Trauma sends four messages to children:

1. Your world is no longer safe.
2. Your world is no longer kind.
3. Your world is no longer predictable.
4. Your world is no longer trustworthy.

If children or teens are involved in a disaster of any kind, they often experience a loss of innocence. Their entire world becomes less safe and secure. They are forced to face issues of loss and bereavement sooner than adults wanted them ever to have to experience. A disaster or trauma makes them a different person.[6]

The following are characteristics of children who have experienced trauma. These post-traumatic stress disorder symptoms are unique to children:

- Children under the age of four tend to forget their experiences, although a few may remember. Those over this age do tend to remember the experiences vividly, whereas adults often deny reality or repress it.
- Most children do not experience the numbing common to adults. Yet if the trauma is parental abuse, they do.
- A child's school performance usually is not impacted by acute trauma for as long a time as adults' work performance is impacted.
- With a child, play and reenactment increases in frequency. And with a child, you will find frequent time distortions.[7]

How to Help a Child Cope

What do children need in a trauma? An abundance of them need to be encouraged just to be patient with themselves. Most of all, they need to know it is all right to feel and express feelings.

Attempt to return children to the world of childhood as soon as possible. They need the routine of school, recreation, bedtime, sports, church, clubs, parties, and so on. Children respond better when they regain the environment that gives them back the security of routine. Children need to be given permission to be children again. Children need to do their usual playing and learning.[8]

When a Child Does Not Cope

The following are some warning signs that indicate a child is not coping well:

- A child consistently does not want or refuses to go to school, or the child's grades drop and do not recover.
- A child loses all interest or pleasure in what he or she used to enjoy.
- A child talks about hurting or killing himself or herself.
- A child hears or sees things other people do not.
- A child cannot eat or sleep enough to remain healthy.[9]

If there is a major upset or tragedy in your community, there are some steps you can take to reduce your child's worry or anxiety:

1. Maintain your daily routines as much as possible, such as mealtime, bedtime, and activities because this is reassuring to a child.

2. Be sure to limit television viewing. Turn it off. When you need to watch, do it by yourself. Many children cannot understand or process what they see on television.

3. Talk about what has occurred, including the various feelings people experience. If a child does not verbalize his concern, he is probably talking to himself about it, and he is not an expert. Encourage your child to talk or write about the tragedy, or draw.

4. When your child asks questions, be honest in your answers. When bad things happen, talk about them. But remember: You probably will not have all the answers. Often the best response to the "Why?" question is, "I wish I knew the answer to why, but right now I don't." Be objective, but share your feelings, too.

5. Use the situation to teach about fear, worry, and anxiety. Let your child know it is all right to have all the various feelings when problems occur in life.

6. Listen to your child with your eyes, as well as with your ears. His behavior will tell you much about his life. Distress signs include nightmares, inability to sleep, irritability, tantrums, or clinginess. If your child has been previously traumatized and now experiences another major life upset, he is more prone to develop anxiety.

7. Always give reassurance. You are there for your child. God is there for him. Other people are there to help him, too. And do not overprotect him. Some parents keep information from their children. But if there are problems or danger, children need to know. They will find out eventually, and it is best coming from you.

8. Be sure to ask for help when you need it or do not know what to do or say.[10]

Know When to Seek Professional Help

Parents often wonder, "When are my child's fears so intense that professional help is warranted?" The following questions will help you evaluate the level of your child's fears.

- Does your child have an abundance of fears? Is he or she afraid of just about everything?

- Is there any fear that is intense enough to interfere with the entire family's functioning and activities?

- Do your child's fears interfere with any social relationships or schoolwork?

- Is your child an unhappy child in general?

- Do your child's fears drive other people up the wall? For instance, some kids are afraid of bugs to the extent that they refuse to enter any room unless someone has checked it out. One child I know had to check the doors and windows every 15 minutes to make sure they were locked.

- Is your child fearful or worrisome but cannot let you know what is bothering him or her?

- Is there any chronic physical condition such as colitis, asthma, ulcers, hypertension, or headaches that seem to be triggered by emotional stress?

- Have any fears intensified or continued over the past year?

- Have you tried to help your child, but with no success?

- Are there any major family difficulties, such as abuse, drug or alcohol problems, marital problems, etc?

A definite "yes" answer to one of these questions and a qualified "yes" to several others indicates that professional help may be a wise choice.[11] Check with your pastor for references or ask your family physician.

9
Children Get Depressed, Too!

Ted is not behaving like a healthy nine-year-old. He has been spending more and more time in his room, either lying on his bed or watching TV. Every now and then he will complain about being bored, but when someone invites him to play, he refuses. Whenever his parents say something to encourage him, he responds with, "Yeah, sure. If you only knew."

What is wrong with Ted? Ted is depressed. Yes, even children become depressed, especially if they have experienced a loss.

Fred is an active three-year-old (at least until last week). Now he seems to mope around with a long face. He shows no interest, despite his mother's efforts to involve him in play. He is not ill. He just does not seem to care anymore.

Can toddlers become depressed? A few years ago specialists realized that preschoolers could experience true depressive feelings. Because young children are unable to verbalize their emotions clearly, their depression is very difficult to diagnose. Parents often excuse listless or tearful episodes as the normal ups and downs of growing up.[1] But the fact is even newborns can show signs of being depressed.

How common is depression among children? One study indicated that as many as eight percent of preschool-age children experience significant depression, and as they get older, their chances of becoming depressed actually increase.[2]

Most depression in childhood goes away quickly, but some children suffer from the more serious, disabling type of depression as well. This chronic type of depression seems to evolve for no apparent reason, or it is out of proportion to whatever triggered it.

The difficulty is that even concerned parents can be so distracted by their own marriages, occupations, or daily responsibilities that they miss the warning signals of their depressed child. They also do not recognize the events that can cause depression.

Why Do Children Become Depressed?

Many factors can trigger depression in children. Divorce remains the leading cause with its multiplicity of losses. Some of the other more common culprits are:

- a physical defect or illness
- malfunction of the endocrine glands
- a lack of affection, creating insecurity
- a lack of positive feedback or encouragement
- death of a parent
- divorce, separation, or parental desertion
- sibling favoritism
- relationship problems between child and stepparent
- financial problems in the family
- a sensitivity to punishment
- a move or change of schools[3]

Most of these center around loss, don't they?

Children often become depressed because of a loss. Sudden loss is particularly hard on children, leaving them feeling out of control and floundering. On the other hand, a gradual loss that can be prepared for is easier for children to manage.

Often depression is heightened if what is lost is perceived as necessary and irreplaceable. In his book *Unveiling Depression in Women* (Revell, 2002), Dr. Archibald Hart describes four different types of loss:

> *Abstract losses* are intangible, such as the loss of self-respect, love, hope, or ambition. Our mind perceives these losses, and we may feel we have experienced them. At times the loss may be real, but it may not be as bad as we feel it is.
>
> *Concrete losses* involve tangible objects—a home, a car, a parent, a close friend, a photograph, or a pet. We could feel and see the object prior to the loss.
>
> *Imagined losses* are created solely by our active imaginations. We think someone doesn't like us anymore. We think people are talking behind our backs. Children often excel at this. Their self-talk focuses on negatives and may not be based on fact.
>
> The most difficult type of loss to handle, however, is the *threatened loss*. This loss has not yet occurred, but there is the real possibility that it will happen. To a child, waiting for the results of a physical exam, or waiting to hear from the relatives to see if he can go to their farm for the summer, carries the possibility of loss. Depression occurs because, in this type of loss, the child is powerless to do anything about it. In a sense, he's immobilized.[4]

If your child is sad or depressed, look for a loss.

Signs of Depression

What does a depressed child look like? How can you know if your child is really depressed and not just sad about something that has happened? We first need to understand the distinction between depression and sadness. The feeling of sadness is less intense than that of depression; it does not last as long, nor does it interfere with day-to-day functioning. Depression causes us to function at 50 percent of normal, and this lower functioning intensifies our feelings of depression. That is a key sign.

A depressed child feels empty. He cannot fully understand what is happening within, but he does know something is wrong.

Below is a composite of the depressed child. Your child probably will not display all these symptoms:

1. Your child may appear sad or depressed. We call this apathy, and it can be expressed in several ways. He might appear restless but does not become involved in activity, may decline to do things he usually enjoys, preferring to be alone or simply daydream. Apathy in a child is a symptom of internal stress.

2. A prominent feature of childhood depression is withdrawal and inhibition. We call this listlessness. Your child may look bored, or often even appears to be ill. Some even become mute. He just will not talk.

3. A depressed child may display physical symptoms, often complaining of headaches, stomachaches, dizziness, insomnia, or eating and sleeping disturbances. These symptoms are called depressive equivalents.

4. A depressed child looks discontented and seems to experience very little pleasure from life.

5. Many depressed children feel rejected and unloved. They withdraw from any situation that may disappoint

them. They fear and expect rejection and protect themselves from it.

Depressed children feel unimportant. The method of expression differs from child to child, but depressed children feel they are less valuable than others. These feelings of inadequacy and low self-esteem may appear in the following ways:

- Quitting a club or ball team because he sees himself as insignificant. ("They'll never miss me.")
- Failing to reach out to help other people for fear of rejection. ("She doesn't want my help.")
- Rejecting affection because of a feeling of unworthiness. ("She can't really love me.")
- Deliberately breaking rules because he thinks following them will lead to failure. ("Other people expect too much of me. They won't like it when I fail.")
- Failing to recognize that mistakes and failures can be corrected. ("I'll never get it right.")
- Refusing to admit to a mistake or failure to save face. ("Why do I always lose?")
- Rejecting the need to learn or grow. ("What difference will it make if I know that or not?")
- Unwillingness to share with other people. ("I rarely get anything worthwhile, so why should I share it? I'm going to keep it all for me.")
- Blaming other people for difficulties and problems. ("Other people try to make my life hard.")
- Rejecting spiritual teachings that could help. ("Why would God love me? I don't believe it.")[5]

6. When a depressed child speaks, she is negative about herself and everything in her life. She draws conclusions

based on her negative mind-set rather than on facts. This further reinforces her feelings of depression.

7. A depressed child will show unusual levels of frustration and irritability. When your child fails to reach his goals, he will be especially hard on himself, commenting disparagingly about his abilities and value.

8. A depressed child looks for comfort and support from other people, but when she receives it, refuses to be comforted and encouraged.

9. Some children will mask their feelings of despair by clowning and acting foolish. Provocative children are less likely to appear in need of comfort and support, so the depression can often continue undetected.

10. Some children demonstrate drastic mood swings when depressed. One minute they appear to be "up," and the next minute they are in the pit of despair. These children tend to believe that if they are "good" enough and work hard enough, life will turn around for them.

11. The depressed child may become the family scapegoat. His behavior can elicit anger, and parents might label him a "problem child." With this label, the depression continues and the child may begin to live up to this classification.

12. The depressed child may tend to be passive, excessively dependent, and assume parents automatically know her needs. Because it is impossible to read a child's thoughts, her needs go unmet. She may become angry and respond in passive-aggressive ways.

13. Depressed kids tend to be overly sensitive, hard on themselves, and self-critical. They create unreasonable goals for themselves, and blame themselves when they fail to attain them.

14. Some depressed children will become aggressive and obsessive in order to cope with how badly they feel.

Depressed children will not exhibit all these characteristics, but when some of them exist, do not just assume the child is misbehaving.[6]

Many children experience depression because they are having difficulties dealing with other people. The strongest need a child has is to belong—to be part of a family and social group. Children who are having problems developing positive relationships are in crisis and can become depressed. Again, they have experienced a loss.

Depression can also result from a traumatic incident. In such cases, the depressed feelings are usually short-lived, and the child soon returns to normal. Following are situations that may not be bothersome to us as adults, but can cause temporary depression in a child:

- failing an exam or a class
- being overlooked for a desired position
- performing poorly in an organized activity, such as Little League, T-ball, or gymnastics
- inability to find someone with whom to play
- being reprimanded or punished
- arguing with a parent, sibling, or friend
- losing a favorite object or a pet
- being denied a request
- entering puberty
- moving from one home to another or losing friends

While these situations cause only short-term depression, circumstances that seem to have no end can leave a child emotionally drained and less resilient. It is clear that the development of childhood depression is influenced by a number of different factors.

This is why no one person or thing can be blamed for the illness if it does occur. For each child, a unique combination of influencing factors may, if left unaddressed, develop into clinical depression. This is why practicing depression prevention at home is so important.

Below is a summary of risk factors that can generate long-term depression in a child based on the influencing factors just discussed. Take a moment to think about your own family in light of these risk factors:

- having a prior clinical depressive episode
- having a depressed parent
- experiencing the death of a loved one
- having low-level depressive symptoms
- experiencing a recent major loss (such as parental divorce or change of location)
- having a family history of clinical depression or drug and alcohol abuse
- having a diagnosis of attention deficit disorder (inactive or hyperactive type), obsessive-compulsive disorder, oppositional defiant disorder, conduct disorder, or an anxiety disorder
- having a history of abuse or trauma
- having a history of chronic or serious medical problems
- living in a family that frequently fights or is violent
- living with acute or chronic stress in the environment
- habitually interpreting life events negatively (pessimism)[7]

Aside from experiencing an episode of depression, the most serious risk factor for a child is having a depressed parent. In fact, some studies indicate that a child of a depressed parent has a 41 to 77 percent chance of experiencing depression or some other psychiatric or behavioral disturbance.[8] This statistic is not due to genetics alone. The *Harvard Mental Health Letter* puts pure hereditability at 50 percent for unipolar depression.[9] It is higher for bipolar depression. The other 50 percent is due to environmental influences. Parents pass on to their children ways of thinking and behaving that encourage and sustain depression.[10]

A depression-prone child can interpret a parent's response as a reinforcement of his negative worth. For example:

- Frequent criticism
  Your child's interpretation: "I can't do anything right."

- Lack of individual attention from parent
  Your child's interpretation: "I'm not important."

- Harsh or angry words from parents
  Your child's interpretation: "I make other people feel upset."

- Parents' failure to acknowledge accomplishments
  Your child's interpretation: "The things I do don't count."

- Parents focusing on negative or upsetting behavior
  Your child's interpretation: "Everyone expects me to be bad."

- Parents' failure to keep promises
  Your child's interpretation: "No one cares if I'm disappointed."

Over time, continuous negative experiences like these contribute to feelings of low self-worth, which can lead to depressed feelings.[11]

There is another type of depression that is often overlooked. An illness as old as mankind is what is called a bipolar disorder. It is considered a neglected public health problem. And it is more common than we think. It is estimated that one-third of all of the children who are being diagnosed with attention-deficit disorder with hyperactivity are actually suffering from early symptoms of bipolar disorder. And this number is more than one million children. It is also thought a third of the 3.4 million children who first seem to be suffering with depression will go on to manifest the bipolar form of a mood disorder.[12]

Some people have referred to bipolar as the manic-depressive or high-low disorder. But children rarely fit the typical bipolar pattern. Their illness seems to be more chronic, and they cycle back and forth with a few times of wellness in between.

Most bipolar children have certain temperamental and behavioral traits in common. They tend to be inflexible, oppositional, and irritable, and experience periods of rage. Their tantrums can last for hours. They rarely show their raging side to the outside world.

If hyperactivity, irritability, shifting moods, and long-lasting temper tantrums coincide, and if there is alcoholism and/or mood disorder in the family background, the possibilities for this problem are high.

These children, right from infancy, slept erratically and were difficult to settle. Some are called the "wide-eyed" babies of the nursery.

Many of these children are precocious and bright—doing everything early and with intensity. They are on a different time schedule than the rest of the world. They also have an extreme inability to be separated from their mother.

Many of these children struggle with sleeping. They wake up screaming because of nightmares. Many children wake up just before the monster or animal gets them. But bipolar children do not. And the intensity of the imagery of their dreams tends to come out in their daily conversation. Accompanying the night terrors is an intense fear of death and annihilation. One author said, "Nighttime is terrifying for the bipolar child, but daytime becomes something of a nightmare for both the child and his or her family as rages begin to erupt."[13] Bipolar children seem to have no control whatsoever over their rage.

Their behavior is often oppositional. They do not have the flexibility to move from one activity to the next. They are very sensitive to all kinds of stimuli: visual, odors, and touch. They always seem to be out of sync. They have difficulty getting along with their peers; they overreact to temperature changes, and crave carbohydrates and sweets. This does not sound like a very pleasant way to live.

Let's return to their cycling pattern. Bipolar children usually cycle rapidly from depression to manic and back again. This pattern can be over days or several times a day. Their moods can shift constantly during the day, and sometimes they can get trapped in the switching process. This is a troublesome set of feelings for a child or adolescent. Can you imagine how difficult it is for a child to function while bouncing from one pole to the other?

Fortunately, more and more research about this disorder is occurring. There are medications that can stabilize these children. (If you feel this brief description describes your child, please read further, especially in *The Bipolar Child* by Demitri and Junie Papolos.)[14]

How You Can Help Your Depressed Child Now

Most parents do not know what to do at this time. What can you say to your depressed child?

Seven-year-old Katy would begin to cry at the drop of a hat. She constantly made negative statements about herself. She talked about being ugly (which was far from the truth), about how other people did not like her (her friends called every day), and about how she could not do anything right (she was a straight-A student). This had been going on for a month. No matter what her parents said or did, she seemed to get worse rather than better.

A good place to start is for her parents to communicate that they care for Katy, want to be with her, and will be available to her.

Conveying acceptance is also important. There is healing in physical touch. An arm around your child's shoulder, a pat on the back, or holding your child's hand can communicate comfort and acceptance. But by all means, be honest and tell your child, "I don't really understand all that you're going through, but I'm trying—and I'm here to help you."

If your child's despair over a loss or trauma is overwhelming because of what he saw or witnessed, he may need to find a way to forget the experience. If so, you can expect to hear, "I don't remember" or "I don't want to talk about it." Or he may change the subject or try to distract you by acting out in some way. Have you ever heard your child say the phrase, "It wasn't anything" or "It was no big deal"? Or your child may not say anything at all.

Had you ever considered that depression sends a message to the person who is depressed? It is not always easy to hear or to accept. But it is there for a purpose, and the message is about something in the child or adolescent that must change before he can feel better.

As a parent, it is important to hear your child's or adolescent's thoughts and feelings about himself. Negative thoughts about himself invariably accompany depression in a child or adolescent. If he says, "I'm so stupid," "I can't do anything," "Why bother?" "I'll never change," all of these thoughts are hopeless thoughts. The good news is that hopeless thoughts can be changed either through your help or the assistance of a counselor.[15]

It is important that you listen in order to pick up and identify hopeless thoughts and beliefs. When you hear them, do not discount them, but get your child to classify and amplify them. You can do this by making guesses. If your child complains about being picked on at school, you could ask:

> Parent: "What does getting picked on at school make you think about yourself?"
>
> Child: "I don't know."
>
> Parent: "Lots of times when kids are getting picked on, they start to believe bad things about themselves. They start to think they are rejects or that nobody will ever like them."
>
> Child: "I don't think anybody will ever like me."[16]

Your job is to assist your child in escaping the thoughts and feelings that are controlling him. And this is best done by following guidelines that have been established by Dr. Douglas Riley:

> Just sitting there and listening, limiting your comments to brief questions and probes to help you find out more about what a child is thinking and feeling, is the hardest skill to learn when you are attempting to help. It is the most important skill, however, because the willingness to keep your comments and questions to a minimum is what often allows a child to talk and arrive at his own solution. Without realizing it, most of us put tremendous pressure on ourselves to come up with solutions for every imaginable problem children might present to us. While it feels nice to be the source of solutions, giving solutions too quickly prevents children from working through the process of discovering their own solutions.[17]

He calls this approach listening to your child with a fascinated ear:

> There are several other attributes to the fascinated ear. Listening with the fascinated ear requires that you be willing to suspend your own viewpoint long enough to learn about your child's viewpoint. You are guaranteed to never learn anything about your children if you just assume they think like you.
>
> There is nothing implied in suspending your own viewpoint that says you must agree with what your child says. If you don't take the time to listen fully and show your child that you are interested in her opinions, she will sense that you don't really care about what she thinks. Once she comes to that opinion, she probably won't give you a chance to engage her in the type of talk that can help correct her mistaken beliefs.
>
> Listening with a fascinated ear also requires that you not take your child's depressed mood and behavior personally. Children and teenagers often express depression through cranky, aggressive behavior. Depressed children and teens can be explosive and out of control because they are so frustrated with the way they see their lives going. If you get swept up into their mood, you yourself can begin to yell, scream, and shout. While your yelling might make your depressed child become quiet, she becomes so only out of fear. By yelling, you have shown her that now no one is in control.
>
> Another attribute of the fascinated ear is communicating to your child that she is free to tell you anything about how she is feeling and thinking without you going into full-blown panic. You will be rightfully frightened if your daughter tells you that she wants to kill herself. But if you *show* that you are overly frightened, it may make her even more frightened about what she is going through and convince her that no one can handle the problems she is facing.[18]

No one would argue that bad things happen to good people. From the simple disappointment of breaking a treasured toy to the catastrophic loss of a loved one, adversity is a part of life. Adversity is also frequently depression's trigger. For most children and adolescents, a depressive episode usually follows a major disappointment. Such children have often experienced a family breakup, family relocation, rejection by peers, and even being bullied in school. Indeed, failures to make the baseball team, breakup of a romantic relationship, and relocation of a best friend have all been implicated as triggers for adolescent suicide.

It is important to remember then, that reducing the risk for depression begins with preparing children to deal with adversity.[19]

Here are some practical suggestions to help you understand and deal with the problem of depression. How closely you follow these will depend upon the intensity and duration of the depression. If your child is experiencing short-term depression and still functioning, certain suggestions will not apply. However, if the depression has lasted quite a while and your child is not eating, sleeping, or functioning on a normal level, you will apply more of these guidelines to the situation.

1. *Help your child learn to express depressed feelings.* Keep in mind that depression robs people of the ability to govern their thinking and emotions. If your depressed child just stares, ignores greetings, or turns away from you, remember that he does not want to act that way. He is not trying to punish you. A severely depressed child cannot control himself any more than you could walk a straight line after twirling around 25 times.

Your child needs to talk about the problems that depress her, but she may avoid doing so. Why? She may think you are not interested, that her problems will seem insignificant to you, or it may be difficult for her to bring up the topic. This is when your availability becomes crucial to your child's survival. Enough time needs to be spent with your child to allow for informal talks that open the door to more serious discussions.

When your child does begin to talk about his or her feelings, several important guidelines should be followed. They are:

- Understand what is being said from your child's point of view. His interpretation of matters (which might be considerably different from yours) is important because his beliefs will largely determine what he does in the future.

- Your nonverbal expressions should indicate a genuine interest in what your child is saying. Avoid anything that might distract you from focusing directly on your child. Lean down so you are on his or her level or sit on the floor.

- Use gentle, open-ended questions to gather information from your child. Avoid implying wrongdoing or guilt in your tone.

- Withhold giving your opinions, information, or advice until your child is ready for it. Let him decide whether he wants you to listen or offer suggestions.

- Control your own emotions. It will help your child maintain composure. A power struggle at this point could serve to just intensify your child's feelings.

- Do not try to fill every moment with words. Silence can allow your child to organize his thoughts.

- Watch your child's nonverbal expressions. Look for the feelings that lie beneath your child's words.

- Allow for disagreement. Your child's perspective may be different than yours.[20]

Most of us as parents have a difficult time coming up with what to say. It is not an everyday occurrence, so it stretches our ability to say something helpful. Here are some suggestions:

- "I am so sorry this happened."
- "I'm glad you're okay, even though it was upsetting."
- "Remember when you broke a bone? Eventually it healed. Your heart will heal in time as well, but it will probably take longer than you want."
- "Sadness is what anyone would feel after something like this."
- "You would like to forget this. We all would. It's too painful to forget right now."
- "It's all right to cry."
- "Your feelings will change from day to day. Sometimes they're all mixed together."
- "Even adults sometimes feel confused about their feelings."
- "I'd like to make your pain go away, but I can't."
- "Sometimes you forget and sometimes it comes back again."
- "Remember when the dentist put Novocain in your mouth to pull your tooth? It felt numb. Sometimes after something like this, you feel numb."[21]
- Ask your child, "Which of these feelings would you like to talk with God about?" and "How would you like Jesus to help you at this time?" One of the promises of Scripture that can be shared is Isaiah 25:8: "And the Lord GOD will wipe tears away from all faces" (NASB).

2. *Watch out for the possibility of suicide.* You may be shocked by this, but children do commit suicide. The family of any

depressed person should be aware of the possibility of suicide. Any suspicions of suicide should be taken seriously. Unfortunately, the incidence of suicide is on the rise, and a child who expresses utter hopelessness for the future may be at risk. If he is able to talk about his suicidal thoughts or plans, it helps bring them out into the open, as well as solicit your support and help.

3. *Consult with your pediatrician.* Certain physical problems can cause depressed feelings. When a child suffers from long-term depression, it is important to consult your pediatrician for possible causes and treatments.

4. *Give support and make adjustments.* The whole family needs to be informed and coached when one of its members is depressed. Ask each person to avoid conflicts, put-downs, and unrealistic expectations. Confrontation and strong discipline should be suspended until stability is restored.

5. *Do not avoid your depressed child.* Avoiding the depressed child further isolates her and worsens the problem. Do not allow yourself to feel guilty and somehow responsible for her depression. Remember, while someone may contribute to another person's problems from time to time, no one person is responsible for another's happiness.

6. *Realize that your depressed child is a hurting child.* Do not tell a depressed child to "just snap out of it." Avoid offering simple solutions like, "Just pray about it" or "Read your Bible more." And never imply that a child is using depression to solicit sympathy. To a depressed child, emotional pain is as intense as—if not more intense than—physical pain.

7. *Empathize rather than sympathize with your child.* Sympathy only reinforces someone's feelings of hopelessness. Statements such as "It's awful that you're depressed" and "You must feel miserable" tend to encourage helplessness and low self-esteem. Instead, let

the child know you have had similar experiences and you know these feelings will pass. Help is available.

8. *Reconstruct your child's self-esteem.* One of the most important steps a parent can take is to help rebuild a child's self-esteem, because when depression occurs, self-esteem tends to crumble. A depressed child does not understand his value as God's creation and the extent of God's love for him. Because of this, he doubts everyone's love as well.

Because a depressed child is unwilling to participate in normal activity, it will not be easy to involve him in opportunities that reinforce self-worth. It might be better to just get the child involved without a lot of discussion. Involve him in activities you know he enjoys, and in which he has experienced success. Focus his attention on his accomplishments. Do not let your child's apathy discourage you. Remember, your child is cautious right now and lacks enthusiasm for life. In time, his excitement will return.[22]

9. *Watch your child's diet.* A depressed child may have no appetite, but nutrition is still important. Do not let food become another "issue" by harping on it or using guilt to get your child to eat. Instead, explain to your child that, hungry or not, it is important to eat. Sit with your child and try to make mealtimes an enjoyable family event.

10. *Keep your child busy.* To the severely depressed child, physical activity is more beneficial than mental activity. Your child will tend to reinforce his depression by avoiding other people, withdrawing from normal activities, not eating well, and offending friends. For this reason, you may run into resistance, so you will need to take charge of planning your child's activities. If he has lost interest in things he usually enjoyed, remind him of the fun he has had in the past, and then gently but firmly insist that he become involved. Do not ask him if he wants to do something—

he will probably decline. And do not allow yourself to become frustrated and say something like, "You're going with me because I'm sick and tired of you feeling sorry for yourself." Instead you might say something like, "I know you haven't been feeling well, but you are entitled to some fun. I think you might like this once we get started. I would like to share this activity with you."

Use any activity your child enjoys, and be aware that you may need to schedule his entire day for him. By getting him involved, you help him begin to break destructive behavior patterns and gain energy and motivation.

11. *Never tease or belittle your child for a lack of self-confidence.* Neither showcase nor ignore low self-esteem. It is a common problem of depression and must be faced. Do not argue about or participate in your child's self-pity, but present the illogical nature of her self-disparagement. Remind her of past accomplishments and help her focus on her abilities. If she says, "I can't do anything," gently name her skills and talents. In time, as her confidence builds, she will begin to overcome her sense of helplessness.

Remember this: If your child experiences depression, see it as a message system telling you that something is wrong and that you need to take action to find the cause.

Suggested Reading

The following will help you grow in your knowledge and understanding of depression:

> *Winning Over Your Emotions* by H. Norman Wright, Harvest House Publishers (1998)
>
> *Why Do I Feel This Way?* by Brenda Poinsett, NavPress (1996)

To help your child deal with grief, see *It's Okay to Cry* by H. Norman Wright, Waterbrook Press (book and workbook, 2004).

10

How Your Child's Identity Affects His/Her Emotions

Every child has an opinion of himself, whether he spends a lot of time thinking about it or not. We all have a map we consult—the mental picture of our self-identity. You do and so do I. And so does your child. It is the "I am" of each person. A child either feels good about himself, or he dislikes, or even hates himself.

Where does this self-identity come from? How does it develop? The image a child has of himself is built upon clusters of memories. Very early in life he begins to form concepts and attitudes about himself, other people, and the world. His self-concept is actually a cluster of attitudes about himself, some favorable and some unfavorable. His mind can never forget an experience. He may not be conscious of it, but it is still there.

To use a simple illustration, your children enter life carrying two containers: one in their left hand and one in their right. There is a plus sign on one container, and it collects all the positive information your children receive about themselves. There is a minus sign on the other container, which holds all the negative information (this includes sarcastic remarks, put-downs, looks of rejection, snubs, cruel statements, etc.).

If children gather more positives than negatives, they travel through life able to be productive and to experience joy and satisfaction. But if they collect more in the negative container than in the positive, they move through life off balance. Their identity and sense of self-worth can become distorted, and they struggle to gain their equilibrium. Often this is reflected in their anger, fear, and sadness.

Your child has memories of situations in which he feels valuable and important, and of others that are not so pleasant. He may have experienced the pain of being rejected in front of a class at school or of you scolding him in front of his friends. Or maybe he spent hours building something, only to have it not work or other people criticize it. He may have walked into a new school and no one talked to him for several days. Memories, both good and bad, form his identity. And these memories can feed the emotions.

Years ago I visited an old-fashioned carnival fun house with a hall of mirrors. It was a hilarious experience. Some of the mirrors made us look fat and squat, while others made us appear as thin as a thermometer. The mirrors reflected countless distorted images everywhere we looked. Finally, at the end was a regular mirror that reflected our normal image.

Some people pass through life never perceiving their normal image. They live with constant self-distortions. These distortions filter messages and comments that would make their personal evaluation accurate. Some of our mirrors distort us by reducing our value. Other mirrors distort us by overestimating our value.

The Scriptures reflect us as we really are. But too often we forget or neglect consulting *this* reflection. We need a constant reminder of who we really are. It is not our evaluation of ourselves that counts, nor that of our friends or parents. God's evaluation is what brings clarity to the mirror. And your children need this.

What reflects your children's identity? What is the origin of their identity? For most, an important influence is the relationship they have with you, their parents. A parent's love is the most important source of who they are. Children who do not experience love and acceptance from their parents have difficulty loving or accepting love from other people. Because they never felt the commitment of their parents, they also have trouble making commitments to other people. They move through life searching for love and commitment. Their need is insatiable—they can never get enough love and commitment. Or they live in fear of losing the love they have, while at the same time they behave in a way that pushes people away and this angers them. Still other children are not willing to risk rejection, so they never become involved in relationships that could provide the love and commitment they crave. They live in fear. This is why parents play such a significant role in their children's development of identity.

Our identity, worth, and value come because God created us, and because we have true identity through Jesus Christ. The foundation for our self-identity is theological. We have been created by the hand of God and in His image. There may be days when we do not feel like that is true, especially if it has been a particularly difficult day. But, nonetheless, it is a fact. When your child grasps this truth, he can handle his emotions so much better. Let's consider this further.

All of us were created in God's likeness (see Genesis 1:26). But how are we made like God?

God created Adam and Eve with an inherent goodness. They were not morally neutral. God was pleased with them, for Genesis 1:31 says, He "saw all that He had made, and behold, it was very good" (NASB). But then Adam and Eve sinned. When sin entered the world, it marred our God-image but did not destroy it. And thus the God-image is the basis of our value, worth, and dignity. (Our God-Image was restored through the sacrificial blood of Jesus on the cross.) That is why we can respond to our children in ways that will help them develop a positive and healthy identity. Your child is *worthy*. Regardless of his or her age, your child is a product of God's handiwork.

Take a look at your children some night while they are sleeping and read Psalm 139:1-6,13-18 aloud. What does this passage tell you about the worth of both you and your children to God?

> O LORD, you have searched me and you know me. You know when I sit and when I rise; you perceive my thoughts from afar. You discern my going out and my lying down; you are familiar with all my ways. Before a word is on my tongue you know it completely, O LORD. You hem me in—behind and before; you have laid your hand upon me. Such knowledge is too wonderful for me, too lofty for me to attain....
>
> For you created my inmost being; you knit me together in my mother's womb. I praise you because I am fearfully and wonderfully made; your works are wonderful, I know that full well. My frame was not hidden from you when I was made in the secret place. When I was woven together in the depths of the earth, your eyes saw my unformed body. All the days ordained for me were written in your book before one of them came to be. How precious to me are your thoughts, O God! How vast is the sum of them! Were I to count them, they would outnumber the grains of sand. When I awake, I am still with you (NIV).

God wants your children to grow up realizing that their worth and value have been decreed not by this world, but by God Himself!

The Role of Your Child's Identity

Why is your children's identity so important? Because it is going to affect just about every area of their lives and especially their emotions.

How children feel about themselves affects their attitude. Children with a strong identity have better attitudes about school, friends, home, parents, and church. The higher value children place on themselves, the more they value the people and things in their lives.

A healthy identity affects your children's health. If they feel good about their bodies and value them, they are less likely to abuse them with drugs and alcohol. It is extremely important that our children learn to love and care for their bodies.

Children with a healthy identity tend to be more honest. Those with a distorted sense of self-worth tend to step over the lines of propriety. They rationalize, *If I don't care about myself, why should I care what others think of me? If I'm not important, why is it so important to follow these dumb rules?*

A healthy identity is tied into how well our children get along with other people. Years ago I heard this statement: "*You cannot be happily married to another person unless you are happily married to yourself.*" There is a lot of truth in that statement, because it is difficult to get along with other people if you do not first get along with yourself.

Identity affects schoolwork as well. School will be a problem when a child thinks, *Why bother? What difference does it make?*

I'm dumb and I can't get any attention by working hard. I might as well make a disturbance. At least I can get some kind of attention that way.

Identifying Your Child's Identity

The following two lists give some characteristics of children with positive identities and children with negative identities. Evaluate the identity of your children as you read over these traits.

Children who have a positive identity:

- are happy children
- feel they are liked by peers
- are able to make friends
- are able to tell you some things they are good at
- feel strong and capable
- feel secure in their home
- feel like important people
- are able to give of themselves to other people
- feel good that they are doing their best in school
- do not measure their importance by grades and accomplishments
- feel like important members of their families
- accept their physical appearance and generally like how they look
- attempt new tasks with courage
- show love and kindness to other people
- participate in games with other children rather than just watch
- feel accepted for their uniqueness

Children who have a negative identity:

- may be unhappy much of the time
- may cry, whine, or withdraw
- may not feel liked by their peers
- may find it difficult to make friends
- may feel that they have to compete at home for attention
- may feel that they are in trouble much of the time
- may not know their own special abilities or talents
- may have lots of conflicts with peers or adults
- may not feel like important members of their families
- may not attempt new tasks because they fear failure
- may feel they are only important if they perform well
- do not show love and kindness to other people
- may watch other children playing and do not participate
- may be extremely competitive with other children
- are often mean to other children
- may feel they are a disappointment to other people
- may be afraid to volunteer answers in a group situation
- may be extremely shy
- may worry a lot[1]

What Determines Your Child's Identity?

Children's first self-concepts begin in infancy. Love, acceptance, and a positive environment all contribute to their sense of who they are. Toward the end of their first year, children have started to fashion a mental image of who they are.

Part of the struggle we have as parents is that our own feelings about our children tend to fluctuate. It is easier on some days to be positive, affirming, and loving than it is on other days, such as when we are tired and hassled. Our feelings help to develop our children's sense of worth, confidence, and value. However, sometimes what we do and say tends to hinder this development. Nicknames or labels that parents give their children can linger for years. Christian psychologist and speaker Bruce Narramore describes some of the labels people in a seminar remembered their parents giving them as children. They included words like *tank, motormouth, leather gut, beanpole, pea brain, simple Sally, fat cow's tail, elephant ears,* and *dead daughter.* These kinds of nicknames not only hurt, but they are also damaging. Consider this about labels and nicknames:

> Whenever a child is labeled, an image is written on his mind. Repeated labels influence a child who is shaping an image of himself. Accusations such as "clumsy" or "stupid" become important elements of the child's growing attitude toward himself. Absorbed and stored in his mind, these labels act as a barrier to his development of self-esteem.
>
> Frequently these labels become so deeply embedded in our personality that they continue to exist even when there is no basis for them. A girl who is teased about her looks, for example, may never learn to like her appearance even after she has become a beautiful woman. A man labeled "stupid" as a child may still feel foolish even though he has a string of college degrees and has proved himself in business. The curse of childhood labeling and ridicule was clearly expressed to me by an attractive woman who said, "I don't care how beautiful people think I am. To me, I'm still an ugly girl from the wrong side of the tracks." Childhood ridicule overruled the reassurances of her

friends because a contradictive image had been etched in her mind.

However, each time parents communicate respect, love, and trust to their child, they lay another building block in the foundation of that child's self-esteem. Praise, genuine acceptance, patience, and affirmation go a long way in helping a young child to cultivate a good attitude toward himself. Such responses from parents and other people help to form the roots of the child's self-acceptance.[2]

We hear so much about victimization today: citizens victimized by criminals, spouses victimizing each other in marriages, etc. Many of our children grow up feeling victimized because of the discouraging messages they receive from their parents. I constantly hear about parental victimization from adult children in my counseling, and unfortunately, this contributes to a child's shattered self-identity.

A middle-aged woman told me,

> I felt victimized most of my life. Oh, nothing dramatic happened to me when I was a child. I wasn't physically or sexually abused. But my mother was critical of me so much of the time. And whenever she said something nice, I couldn't believe it because the compliments were surrounded by so many discounting statements. Dad just wasn't available to me. He didn't want to talk or play with me. He was around physically, but I felt emotionally abandoned. I grew up wondering what was so wrong with me to keep him from being part of my life.

Children who grow up receiving discounting messages believe they deserve these messages. They learn to cope by blaming themselves for the criticism, abandonment, and discounting they receive. By the time they reach adolescence and adulthood, they may be relatively free from their parents' critical messages. But they have internalized blame to such an extent that they now discount themselves. They make statements of denial, criticism, and blame to themselves like: *I can't do anything right. What a dummy! I should have done that differently. There must be something wrong with me if the teacher has to show me the same formula over and over.* These statements reflect a self-image in trouble.

We parents sometimes unknowingly set the stage for this to occur in our children. We have no idea how powerfully our words, tone, and actions influence our children. Consider these insights from the Book of Proverbs:

> There are those who speak rashly, like the piercing of a sword, but the tongue of the wise brings healing (Proverbs 12:18).
>
> Death and life are in the power of the tongue, and they who indulge in it shall eat the fruit of it (Proverbs 18:21).
>
> Do you see a man who is hasty in his words? There is more hope for a [self-confident] fool than for him (Proverbs 29:20).

When we ignore our children and deny the severity or importance of their life events, the solvability of their problems, or their ability to succeed, they internalize their feelings and grow up limited and struggling with their identity. When we criticize them, they grow up criticizing and abusing themselves.

Here are several examples of discounting messages that lead to this problem of a shattered self-identity. Can you identify the denial, criticism, abandonment, and abuse in these examples?

- Your child is selecting something at the store to buy with his allowance. You keep saying, "Are you sure that's what you want? Once you buy it, we're not bringing it back."

- You make fun of your child for being afraid of a large dog.
- You berate your child for losing a fish as he was trying to pull it into the boat.
- You tell your child, "You're going to turn out just like your rotten father."
- You ridicule your adolescent son for being bashful around girls.
- You make fun of your child's visible handicap or weakness in front of other children or your adult friends.
- You tell your six-year-old, "I will love you if you're a good boy."
- You say to your child, "If you get good grades and are quiet around the house, Daddy and I won't fight as much."
- You tell your 14-year-old boy, "I don't have time for you when you behave this way. Go to your room until you figure out what's wrong with you."[3]

Children who grow up on a steady diet of these kinds of messages will have an incredible knack for blaming themselves for situations that are not their responsibility. Instead of becoming mature, independent, self-confident individuals, their adult lives will be marked by self-blame, self-doubt, and insecurity.

If you are the conveyor of negative messages to your children, it is very likely that you were the recipient of negative messages from your parents as a child. To some degree, you adopted a discounting self-attitude. However, the pattern can be broken.

The first step of breaking this cycle is to become aware of your own thought patterns. Do you ever deny the existence or severity of a problem in your life? Do you ever deny your ability to solve a personal problem? Are you overly self-critical? Do you blame yourself for situations that are not your responsibility? Do you abuse yourself verbally? How is your own self-identity?

A negative tendency is often so ingrained that it is an automatic response. Bringing it to the surface will take some work on your part, but the results will be worth it. Realize that you are not doing this to increase your guilt or to be hard on yourself. You are simply trying to discover how much of your behavior is motivated by discounting yourself.

One way to determine if this is true for you is to track your responses to the problems you encounter. Ask yourself several times a day, "Am I ignoring a problem which really exists? Am I overreacting to the problem? Have I asked for help in solving the problem? Did I avoid the situation because I didn't think I could solve it?"

The good news about this negative thinking pattern is that it can change; you can break the cycle in your family. But first you must become an explorer of your own attitudes and responses. Once you identify your own thought patterns, you are free to choose alternative nurturing approaches or solutions. What you learn about yourself will help you change your discounting responses toward your children.[4]

Nurturing messages are those which convey to your children something good about themselves. These positive messages do not increase their value; they are already priceless in God's eyes. But nurturing messages increase your children's value in their own eyes, thus opening the door for learning, growth, maturity, independence, and a healthy self-perspective.

We need to nurture our children every day. Casual, spontaneous comments and planned, direct, eye-to-eye statements are equally effective. Nurturing involves giving more affirmation than corrections.

Your pattern for responding to your children can be best summed up in two passages from God's Word. The first is Colossians 3:21: "Fathers, do not provoke or irritate or fret your children [do not be hard on them or harass them], lest they become discouraged and sullen and morose and feel inferior and frustrated. [Do not break their spirit.]"

This translation tells us so clearly the results of discouraging words. The other side is found in 1 Thessalonians 5:11: "Therefore encourage (admonish, exhort) one another and edify (strengthen and build up) one another, just as you are doing."

Encouragement comes through praising. All children need to be praised for their efforts, for improving, and for just being who they are as individuals. Praise your kids when they least expect it. Even young children, who have no vocabulary, will pick up praise from your tone of voice and nonverbal communication. It is your attitude that speaks to them.

One mother said she hugged her infant when he was learning to stand, whether he stood for two, six, or ten seconds. A father said he made it a point to praise his daughter for every effort she made—even if it was only a 20 percent effort. In time, he noticed that she began to become more persistent and did not give up as easily. It is important as a parent that you look for things to praise.

Years ago I worked with a mother who was having difficulty with her child. The mother was concerned because her daughter was demonstrating poor behavior and low self-esteem. I tried an approach that I had never suggested before. Each day the mother was to keep a record of each time she criticized her daughter. I was shocked the next week when she walked into my office and literally threw several sheets of paper at me. "It's not you I'm upset with," she moaned. "It's me. I couldn't believe how many times I criticized my daughter. No wonder she's responding the way she is. She's not the problem. I am."

"How can I respond in a way that will be accepted?" you may ask. How? It is actually quite simple. In place of focusing on the behavior that you do not like or want to eliminate, direct your attention (and theirs) to what it is you want them to do. There is a greater likelihood that your children will change when you focus more on what you want them to do rather than reinforce what they have been doing. If you make a point each day of sharing with your children messages that nurture, it will soon become automatic. It works!

Nurturing shows your children that you believe in their capacity to learn, change, and grow. Nurturing shows that you are aware of the kind of picture you want your kids to have of themselves. Their minds are like computers. Every message you send to them goes into one of the two files: *discounting* or *nurturing*. And the file with the most data will determine how they see themselves. When nurturing occurs on a regular basis, it is difficult for low self-esteem to gain a foothold in your child's mind.

I like the story that Kevin Leman shares about his own experience when he was 12. He was selected as the starting third baseman for his All-Star Little League game. In the third game, the teams battled to a tie, and Kevin's team needed one more out to send the game into extra innings.

A ground ball was hit, and the shortstop threw a perfect toss to Kevin at third base for a force-out. It was a good throw. There was no sun in his eyes. But another player bumped into him and he dropped the ball. It just popped out of his glove, and the other team won the game. He felt totally deflated, and tears began to fill his eyes.

Fortunately, he had a manager who was a wise man and knew how Kevin must be feeling. He walked over to Kevin, put his arm around him, and said, "Kevin, if it hadn't been for you, we never would have made it this far, and I want you to remember that. You've been doing a good job all year, so keep your head up."

Is this how you respond to your children when they mess up? Did you ever have anyone respond to you this way when you were a child and made a mistake? This is nurturing. This is encouragement. This is believing in another person.

Messages that nurture are based on unconditional love, which parents must work at, especially if they grew up in a negative home instead of a nurturing family. But you can rely on Jesus Christ to fill the void in your life with His presence and help you learn how to love unconditionally.

Let's look at two types of nurturing messages that will help develop healthy, self-disciplined children. The first category is affirmations and compliments, given for your children's good behavior and right choices. The second category is nurturing messages of correction for bad behavior and wrong choices.

It is easier for most parents to affirm positive behavior than to deal with negative behavior in a positive way. But we must continually remind ourselves to convey nurturing affirmations and compliments such as:

- "You treat your friends very nicely."
- "You have a wonderful ability with tools."
- "Thanks for doing such a good job on your chores today."
- "Your schoolwork has really improved."
- "I like the way you cleaned your room. Thank you."
- "You're a very special person to me."
- "I'm so glad you're my child."
- "I love you because you deserve to be loved. You don't have to earn it."

- "You make my life more complete just by being you."
- "I'm so glad I have you. You teach me so much about life."

Such affirmations cause kids to realize, *Mom and Dad really love me. They think I'm a lovable person. My needs are important to them. They want to help me face my problems and solve them. What happens to me is very important to them. They trust me to think for myself and make good decisions.*

As you convey nurturing messages, be sure your value judgments are attached to your children's behavior instead of their person. For example, a toddler exploring the family room approaches the television, which is within his reach. Fascinated by the shiny knobs and switches, he reaches out to touch the TV. His mother says, "Don't touch, Joshua. Remember, I said you can look at the television, but you can't touch it. Here are some things you can touch." She jiggles a box of toys. Joshua stands in front of the TV a moment, wrestling with the temptation. Then he turns away toward the toys.

What would you have said to affirm Joshua? Many of us would remark, "Good boy, Joshua!" And if he had touched the TV against his mother's wishes, it would be, "Bad boy, Joshua!" Those kinds of statements are value judgments on Joshua. He soon learns that he is sometimes good and sometimes bad, which confuses his self-perception.

Instead Joshua's mother said, "Good choice, Joshua!" She wants him to learn that he is capable of making good choices for which he is affirmed, and bad choices, for which he is corrected. But Joshua is always regarded and nurtured as a good boy. This subtle, but important distinction can make a world of difference in your children's feelings about themselves.

When your children make wrong choices or misbehave, they need to be corrected. But since we are concerned with nurturing them at all times, corrective messages must be delivered in a positive, affirming way. We do not correct our children to make them feel bad, but to help them discover a better way to do something. Here are a few examples of nurturing statements of correction:

- "Here is a way you can do it that you might like better."
- "It sounds like it's hard for you to accept a compliment. Perhaps you need more practice accepting them, and I need more practice giving them."
- "I'm not sure you heard what I said. Tell me what you heard, and then let me repeat what I said if you heard differently."
- "Listen to the help and care I'm giving you right now."
- "You can't do that any longer, but you can do this instead."
- "That was a poor choice you made, but I have some good ideas you may want to consider for getting back on track."
- "You're not paying attention. Something must be on your mind, because you are so good at listening and thinking. I wonder what it is?"

What steps can you follow to help your children develop a healthy identity? The first step is to teach the Word of God at an early age, focusing on who they are in Christ. Children who grow up with a healthy and accurate understanding of God and how He views them will have a good basis for their identity.

Genesis 1:26-27   I am uniquely created in God's image.

Matthew 5:13   I am the salt of the earth.

Matthew 5:14	I am the light of the world.
Luke 11:9-10	I ask and receive, I seek and find, I knock and the door is opened unto me.
John 8:32	The truth has set me free.
John 14:27	I have peace.
John 17:18	I have been sent into the world.
John 17:22	I have God's glory.
Acts 13:38	I have forgiveness of sins through Christ.
Romans 8:1	I have no condemnation.
Romans 8:32	I have all things.
Romans 12:6	I have been given gifts.
1 Corinthians 2:16	I have the mind of Christ.
1 Corinthians 3:9	I am God's fellow worker; I am God's field, God's building.
2 Corinthians 4:16	My inner self is being renewed day by day.
Ephesians 3:20	I have a power source within me which is able to do exceeding abundantly beyond all that I ask or think.
Philippians 4:7	The peace of God guards my heart and mind.
Philippians 4:13	I can do all things through Him who strengthens me.
2 Timothy 1:7	For God has not given me a spirit of timidity, but of power and love and discipline.
Philemon 6	The knowledge of every good thing is in me.
1 Peter 2:9-10	I am chosen.

One of the most important verses for them to learn is Ephesians 1:4-5 (TLB):

> Long ago, even before he made the world, God chose us to be his very own, through what Christ would do for us; he decided then to make us holy in his eyes, without a single fault—we who stand before him covered with his love. His unchanging plan has always been to adopt us into his own family by sending Jesus Christ to die for us. And he did this because he wanted to!

How do you direct your child's thoughts so he begins thinking about himself in a positive way? One way is through a series of questions or "leading statements" that you weave into your everyday conversations with him. These are simple, and yet in time could have an effect upon his perspective. You could ask: "What was something you did today that you felt good about?" "Tell me about something you really enjoyed today."

Sometimes I run into parents who express concerns over the fact that their children seem unable to handle praise or a compliment. They seem embarrassed and awkward when it is given and appear to discount the praise. For children who are struggling with their identity, this is not uncommon. Some children will disagree with the praise, shrug, ignore the statement, argue with you, or give someone else the credit for what happened.

Accepting criticism is easier for some children, because it reinforces what they believe about themselves. When you were a child did anyone give you guidelines for accepting a compliment or handling praise? Probably not. Most of us were not given any help or, at the most, we were told to just say, "Thank you." Unfortunately, just saying "Thank you" can become so automatic that we do not even hear ourselves saying the words.

Perhaps the best way to teach children how to accept a compliment or praise is by modeling for them our own response to compliments. As children learn to respond appropriately to a compliment (even though they feel uncomfortable and awkward), they will in time feel better about themselves because of these positive responses. Here are some guidelines you can teach your children, and eventually these will become very natural for them:

- Don't ignore the complimenter.
- Don't downgrade the compliment.
- Don't question the motives of the complimenter.
- Don't mock the compliment.
- Don't question the intelligence of the complimenter.
- Don't question the sanity of the complimenter.
- Don't give the credit to someone else.
- Don't shrug.
- Don't look down at the floor.
- Don't turn around.
- Don't walk away.
- Don't look pained.
- Don't look confused.
- Don't say, "Who? Me?"
- Don't whisper.
- Don't mumble.
- Don't say, "You're kidding."
- Don't giggle.
- Don't run for cover.
- Don't say, "But it was an accident."
- Don't say, "But I could have done better."

- Don't say, "But it's no big deal."
- Don't say, "Yes, but…"
- Don't say, "Maybe, but…"
- Don't say, "Okay, but…"[5]

Use statements like "Thank you. I appreciate you telling me that" or "Thank you. I'm glad you noticed and told me" or "Thank you. That helps me to hear that."

When you first begin teaching your children to do this, accept their responses without corrections. They may mumble and even look away. Reinforce and praise all of their efforts. In time, they will be more definite in words and tone and even in their non-verbal expressions. One mother said she made a game out of this approach with her preschooler. She said to her five-year-old, "Janice, I'm going to tell you something that I like about you, and let's see what you can say back to me. I think you'll like this game."

A father used this approach with his eight-year-old son: "Jim, I'm going to give you some compliments and show you a new way to accept them. As you learn this, I think you are going to feel better about yourself."

Most of us have no idea how to accept a compliment correctly. We are afraid that if we agree with the person who complimented us, we will sound conceited. Sometimes just thinking about the compliment can make us feel self-conscious. So we look down at the floor. We turn around. We blush or give a "Who? Me?" look. We do not say, "Thank you." Or if we do, we whisper or mumble it. We give credit to everyone but ourselves. And we question the complimenter's motives (*Why would he be saying that about me? He must want something*) or sanity (*She's crazy if she thinks that*).

Criticism, which reinforces what we believe about ourselves, is easy for us to accept. In fact, it sometimes stays with us for days, weeks, and even years. But praise goes in one ear and out the other. We discount it, ignore it, and disown it.

Some of us feel starved for praise. Ironically, we may be getting all the praise we need, but we just do not hear it. We dismiss it or shrug it off before it can have a positive effect on our identity.

Praise can only make your children feel better about themselves if they learn to accept it. The rules for doing that are pretty simple. You can teach them to your children in a couple of days. But first, you will need to learn them yourself and begin using them in front of your kids. When it comes to accepting praise, what you *do* may affect your kids even more than what you *tell* them. Learning to accept compliments will have a dramatic impact on your children's identity and their emotional response.

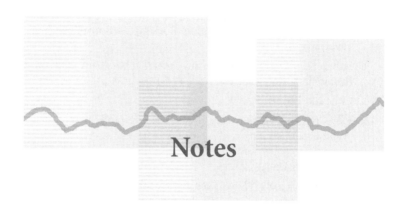

Notes

Chapter 1—The Problem with Anger

1. Dr. Tim Murphy, *The Angry Child* (New York: Three River Press, 2001), p. 50.

2. Murphy, adapted, pp. 44-70.

3. Archibald D. Hart, *Stress and Your Child* (Dallas, TX: Word Publishing, 1992), pp. 110-11.

Chapter 2—Understanding Anger

1. Gary Oliver and H. Norman Wright, *Kids Have Feelings Too* (Wheaton, IL: Victor Books, 1993), pp. 95-96.

2. Gary Hawkins with Carol Hawkins, *Prescription for Anger* (New York: Warner Books, 1988), adapted, pp. 45-51.

Chapter 3—Your Child's Anger

1. Lynn Clark, Ph.D., *SOS Help for Emotions* (Bowling Green, KY: SOS Program and Parent's Press, 2002), adapted, pp. 166-71.

2. Dr. Tim Murphy, *The Angry Child* (New York: Three River Press, 2001), adapted, p. 24.

3. Murphy, p. 25.

4. Murphy, adapted, pp. 28-32.

5. Murphy, adapted, pp. 29-39.

6. Dr. Henry Cloud and Dr. John Townsend, *Boundaries with Kids* (Grand Rapids, MI: Zondervan, 1999), pp. 110-11.

7. Cloud and Townsend, pp. 104-05.

8. Robert J. MacKenzie, *Setting Limits* (Rocklin, CA: Prima Publishing, 1998), adapted, pp. 2-11.

9. Foster Cline, M.D., and Jim Fay, *Parenting with Love and Logic* (Colorado Springs, CO: NavPress, 1990), adapted, p. 62.

10. Cline and Fay, adapted, p. 67.

11. John Gray, Ph.D., *Children Are from Heaven* (New York: HarperCollins Publishers, 1999), pp. 38-40.

Chapter 4—Anger Under Control

1. Aaron T. Beck, *Love Is Never Enough* (New York: Harper & Row, 1988); idea adapted from pp. 270-74 and communication experiments over several years of counseling with couples.

2. Beck, adapted, pp. 274-76.

Chapter 5—How to Help Your Child Deal with Anger

1. Richard Hayman, Ed.D, *How to Say It to Teens* (New York: Prentice Hall, 2001), adapted, p. 20.

2. Dr. Paul Coleman, *How to Say It to Your Kids* (New York: Prentice Hall, 2000), p. 22.

3. Hayman, adapted, pp. 18-19.

4. Elizabeth Verdich and Marjorie Lisovskie, *Take the Grrrr Out of Anger* (Minneapolis, MN: Free Spirit, 2000), adapted, p. 2.

5. Verdich and Lisovskie, adapted, p. 5.

6. Elaine Whitehouse and Warwick Pudney, *A Volcano in My Tummy* (Gabriola Island, BC, Canada: New Society Publishers, 1996), p. 12.

7. Gary Oliver and Carrie Oliver, *Raising Sons and Loving It!* (Grand Rapids, MI: Zondervan, 2001), p. 155.

8. Oliver, pp. 155-57.

9. Coleman, p. 21.

Chapter 6—The Fear of a Child

1. Paul Faxman, Ph.D., *The Worried Child* (Alameda, CA: Hunter House Publishers, 2004), adapted, pp. 9-12.

2. Ibid., adapted, p. 111.

3. Katharina Manassis, M.D., FRCP, *Keys to Parenting the Anxious Child* (New York: Barron's Educational Series), p. 42.

4. Manassis, p. 43.

5. Edward M. Hallowell, *Worry* (New York: Pantheon Books, 1997), adapted, p. 73.

6. Faxman, adapted, pp. 21-22.

7. E.P. Sarafino and J.W. Armstrong, *Child and Adolescent Development* (Glenview, IL: Scott, Foresman, 1980), adapted.

8. E.P. Sarafino, "Children's Fears," in Corsini, R.J., *Encyclopedia of Psychology,* vol. 1 (New York: Wiley and Sons, 1984), adapted.

9. Sarafino, "Children's Fears," adapted, pp. 20-34.

10. Jonathan Kellerman, *Helping the Fearful Child* (New York: W. W. Norton and Co., 1981), adapted, pp. 19-20.

11. Sarafino, "Children's Fears," adapted, p. 36.

12. Sarafino, "Children's Fears," adapted, p. 37.

13. A.H. Buss and R. Ploman, *A Temperamental Theory of Personality Development* (New York: John Wiley & Sons, 1975), adapted.

Chapter 7—Where Do Their Fears Come From?

1. E.P. Sarafino and J. W. Armstrong, "Children's Fears," in Corsini, R. J., *Encyclopedia of Psychology,* vol. 1 (New York: Wiley and Sons, 1984), adapted, 20-34.

2. Sarafino and Armstrong, adapted, pp. 20-34.

3. Ibid.

4. Sarafino, "Children's Fears," adapted, p. 75.

5. Barbara Brooks, Ph.D., and Paula N. Siegal, *The Scared Child* (New York: John Wiley and Sons, 1996), pp. 32-33.

6. Sarafino, "Children's Fears," adapted, p. 75.

Chapter 8—Preparing Your Children to Avoid the Fears of Life

1. Katharina Manassis, M.D., FRCP, *Keys to Parenting the Anxious Child* (New York: Barron's Educational Series), adapted, pp. 24-26.

2. Dylan Tatz, *The Spectator,* p. 19, quoted in Joanne Tortorici Luna, Ph.D., "Collaborations Assessment and Healing in Schools After Large-Scale Terrorist Attacks," *International Journal of Emergency Mental Health* 4, no. 3 (Summer 2002), p. 205.

3. Robert Sandler, social studies teacher, *The Spectator,* p. 16, quoted in Joanne Tortorici Luna, Ph.D., "Collaborations Assessment and Healing in Schools After Large-Scale Terrorist Attacks," *International Journal of Emergency Mental Health* 4, no. 3 (Summer 2002), p. 205.

4. G. Torres, personal communication, March 30, 2001, quoted in Joanne Tortorici Luna, Ph.D., "Collaborations Assessment and Healing in Schools After Large-Scale Terrorist Attacks," *International Journal of Emergency Mental Health* 4, no. 3 (Summer 2002), pp. 205-06.

5. Kendall Johnson, *Trauma in the Lives of Children* (Alameda, CA: Hunter House Publishers, 1988), pp. 72-73.

6. Wendy Zubenko and Joseph Capozzoli, eds., *Children and Disasters* (New York: Oxford University Press, 2002), p. 43.

7. Johnson, *Trauma in the Lives of Children,* p. 63.

8. Zubenko and Capozzoli, pp. 96-97.

9. Zubenko and Capozzoli, p. 99.

10. Paul Faxman, Ph.D., *The Worried Child* (Alameda, CA: Hunter House Publishers, 2004), adapted, pp. 140-42.

11. Sarafino, "Children's Fears," adapted, p. 127.

Chapter 9—Children Get Depressed, Too!

1. *Parents Magazine,* June 1986, adapted, p. 190.

2. Colette Dowling, "Rescuing Your Child from Depression," magazine unknown, January 20, 1992, adapted, p. 47.

3. Brent Q. Hofen and Brenda Peterson, *The Crisis Intervention Handbook* (Englewood Cliffs, NJ: Prentice Hall, 1982), adapted, pp. 21-39.

4. Archibald Hart, Ph.D. and Catherine Hart Weber, P.h.D., *Unveiling Depression in Women* (Grand Rapids, MI: Fleming H. Revell, 2002), pp. 84-85.

5. Frederick F. Flach and Suzanne Draghi Edetait, *The Nature and Treatment of Depression* (New York: John Wiley and Sons, 1975), adapted, pp. 89-90.

6. Dr. William Leo Carter, *Kid Think* (Dallas, TX: Word, Rapha, 1992), adapted, p. 129.

7. Kathleen Panula Hackey, *Raising Depression Free Children* (Center City, MO: Hazelden, 2003), p. 21.

8. Sheryl H. Goodman, and Ian H. Gotlib, eds. *Children of Depressed Parents: Mechanisms of Risk and Implications for Treatment* (Washington, D.C.: American Psychological Association, 2002), p. 3.

9. Richard Harrington, Hazel Fudge, Michael Rutter, Andrew Pickles, and Jonathan Hill, "Adult Outcomes of Childhood and Adolescent Depression," *Archives of General Psychiatry 47* (May 1990), pp. 465-73.

10. Hackey, p. 67.

11. Carter, p. 142.

12. Demitri Papolos, M.D., and Junie Papolos, *The Bipolar Child* (New York: Broadway Books, 1999), adapted, p. 4.

13. Papolos and Papolos, p. 12.

14. Papolos and Papolos, adapted, pp. 7-26.

15. Dr. Douglas A. Riley, *The Depressed Child* (Dallas, TX: Taylor Trade Publisher, 2000), adapted, pp. 3-4.

16. Riley, p. 19.

17. Riley, p. 28.

18. Riley, pp. 31-32.

19. Riley, p. 48.

20. Carter, pp. 134-35.

21. Debra Whiting Alexander, *Children Changed by Trauma* (Oakland, CA: New Harbinger, 1999), adapted, pp. 6-7.

22. Carter, p. 136.

Chapter 10—How Your Child's Identity Affects His/Her Emotions

1. Jean Illsley, Clarke Dawson and Connie Dawson, *Growing Up Again* (New York: Harper and Row, 1989), pp. 17-27.

2. Kevin Leman, *Measuring Up* (New York: Dell Publishing, 1988), adapted, pp. 11-12.

3. H. Norman Wright, *Power of a Parent's Words* (Ventura, CA: Regal Books, 1991), adapted, pp. 142-150.

4. Debora Phillips, *How to Give Your Child a Great Self-Image* (New York: Random House, 1989), p. 59.

5. Phillips, pp. 87-89.